D1744386

9780571045990

WITHDRAWN FROM
TAMESIDE LIBRARIES

The Story of Clothes

The Story of Clothes

by
AGNES ALLEN

with drawings by
AGNES AND JACK ALLEN

FABER AND FABER
24 Russell Square
London

1967

First published in mcmlv
by Faber and Faber Limited
24 Russell Square London W.C.1
Second impression mcmlvii
Third impression mcmlxi
New edition mcmlxvii
Printed in Great Britain by
Latimer Trend & Co Ltd Plymouth
All rights reserved

To
Mabel and George Allen

Contents

1	Man Begins to Clothe Himself	*page* 11
2	Man Learns How to Make Fabrics	18
3	Clothes in Ancient Egypt	25
4	Old Testament Times	35
5	In Crete and Ancient Greece	47
6	Clothes in Northern Europe	60
7	The Reign of the Toga	66
8	In Early Christian Times	76
9	At the Byzantine Court	82
10	The Clothes of the 'Barbarians'	89
11	In the Twelfth and Thirteenth Centuries	99
12	Clothes are Made To Fit	112
13	Sleeves, Hats and Pointed Toes	123
14	Man Becomes Broad and Square	137
15	Bombast, Farthingales and Ruffs	147
16	Cavalier Elegance and Puritan Plainness	165
17	Ribbons and Periwigs	179
18	Coats and Waistcoats Come to Stay	195
19	Hoops and Panniers	207
20	France Imitates Ancient Greece	219
21	The Age of the Crinoline	227
22	What Will Come Next?	243
	Index	253

9

CHAPTER 1

Man Begins to Clothe Himself

Nature has supplied every animal except man with some such covering for his body as fur, feathers, hair, scales, shells or a thick hide. But man has nothing but a thin skin, and for thousands of years human beings must have wandered about the world with no other covering—though the earliest men may perhaps have been hairier than modern man.

If someone were to ask us 'Why did human beings start to cover their bodies with clothes?' most of us would answer 'Why, to keep themselves warm, of course'.

It is only when we begin to think about it a little that we realize that clothes are worn for a great many reasons that have nothing to do with the climate, or with our need for warmth, at all.

For instance, we wear clothes to some extent in order to *decorate* ourselves—to make ourselves, if possible, look more dignified or graceful or picturesque than we are. Even the plainest clothes worn by civilized people have their buttons, belts, collars and so forth arranged in such a way that they form a kind of decoration, and the material itself is of a kind and colour that we think suits us, and is cut or arranged in a way that we think looks nice—though ideas about what looks nice change very much from time to time.

Besides decorating us our clothes have to link us up with the people amongst whom we live. We feel uncomfortable if they do not look 'right'—if they are not similar to those which other people of our age, sex, country and period are wearing. No girl would feel happy if she were sent to school in the kind of clothes her great-grandmother wore, even if the weather was cold and the clothes were warm. And no Englishman would care to walk about London on a hot day dressed as an Ancient Greek, even though he might think that such clothes were cooler and more comfortable than those which are worn by men of the present day.

Our clothes, too, must not only be right for the country and period in which we live, but also for the company we happen to be in at any particular time, or the activity we happen to be engaged in. We might feel quite happy in our own gardens, or on the beach, in a pair of slacks and a grubby shirt or jumper, but we should feel horribly embarrassed if we found ourselves at a reception at Buckingham Palace in such clothes.

So appearance—what we look like—is often as important to us as warmth or coolness when we choose our clothes, whether we are people who care about being fashionable or not.

Clothes, too, have to serve the special purpose of telling other people something about us—who we are, what country we come from, what our position in the world is, even what we can do, or have done in the past. We wear clothes of a certain shape and colour to show that we go to a certain school, or that we are boy scouts or girl guides, or policemen, nurses, soldiers or whatever else it may be. Or we may wear something —probably, nowadays, a medal or badge—to show that we have done some particular thing such as winning the Victoria Cross by a brave action, or been to some particular place such as the shrine of some saint, or that we have become particularly skilful or learned in some way. On special occasions some people wear crowns, robes and other things to show that they are kings, dukes, or something of that kind.

Clothes of a special kind are often worn to show that the wearer has authority or power. The individual wearing them is treated with respect because he occupies a certain office. The judge on the Bench, for instance, might look a very ordinary and unimpressive figure without his wig and gown. Clothes are an essential part of all ceremonial, whether it is connected with religion, the law, parliament, royalty, the fighting forces, the state, or some less important body. How very different our

Queen's Coronation ceremony would have looked without the robes and coronets, the cloth of gold and the ermine.

Sometimes, even in civilized countries, people wear some article of clothing, or some jewel or charm, because they believe that it will bring them luck or protect them from evil or illness, or because it is connected with their religious beliefs.

None of these reasons for wearing clothes—to decorate ourselves, to show our position in the world, for ceremonial purposes, for 'luck', to give ourselves dignity and authority—have anything to do with our need for warmth and protection from the weather. And it is possible that prehistoric man worried even less about keeping his body warm than we do, because civilized people, after having worn clothes for thousands of years, are probably much more sensitive to cold than the men of the Stone Age were.

We know that primitive people who are living now, or were until quite recently, in conditions similar to those in which men lived many thousands of years ago, do not seem to feel the cold as we do.

Charles Darwin, who sailed round the world in the 1830s, wrote an account of the way the native people lived in Tierra del Fuego, the cold land at the southern tip of South America. The shelters made by one tribe were nothing but wind-breaks made by sticking a few broken branches in the ground and thatching them on one side with tufts of grass and rushes. They were only used for a few days at a time, as the Fuegians were constantly moving on from place to place hunting animals and gathering shell-fish. Sometimes they did not even bother to make a windbreak at all, but curled up to sleep on the bare ground, with nothing to shelter them from the cold wind, rain, sleet and snow.

Yet they did not protect themselves with warm clothing. One tribe wore nothing but cloaks made from the skin of an animal called a guanaco. Others wore nothing at all. Darwin describes seeing a group of men and women, all quite naked, fishing in the rain from a canoe off one of the islands, and another day a Fuegian woman, nursing a tiny baby, stood and watched the strangers while sleet fell and melted on her own and her child's naked bodies. Some of the men wore an otter skin or something similar, about the size of a man's handkerchief. This they placed on their backs, and tied it in position with a string round their chests, and they moved the scrap of material from side to side according to the way the wind was blowing.

When Darwin and his friends gave pieces of red cloth to the Fuegians they were delighted—but not because they could use the cloth to make warm clothing. They promptly tore it into strips which they tied round their heads. They valued it as *decoration*.

An old man who acted as spokesman for a group of Fuegians and who was evidently their chief, had something tied round his head to hold a number of white feathers in place. Apparently this was to distinguish him from his followers and make his position clear.

Other explorers and writers besides Darwin have found that such clothes as primitive and savage races wear are often put on for decoration or because the wearer is taking part in some ceremony, and not for warmth. One traveller has described seeing a native put a little short cape over his bare shoulders when he was about to enter a building for a tribal conference, and take it off again when he came out into the open air.

Nearly all savage tribes paint their faces and bodies in some way. Some of them have cuts made in their skins in a certain pattern, which when they heal leave permanent scars. And tattooing, by which a pattern is pricked into the skin and coloured dyes are inserted so that the pattern remains for ever, is a very ancient art indeed. Tiny finely pointed flint tools have been found by archaeologists (the people who make a study of the very distant past) and some of them think that such tools may have been used for tattooing in prehistoric times.

Whether Stone Age men really tattooed and painted their bodies, and, if so, when they started doing so, we can only guess. But we know that many thousands of years ago they began to make necklaces, pendants, bangles, head bands and so on for themselves. The teeth of animals, small bones, and shells, all with holes pierced through them, have been found with the bones of men and women of the Stone Age who lived more than twenty thousand years ago. Beads, too, cut from rods of ivory, or made from pieces of amber and coloured stones, have been found with the tools and implements of Stone Age man.

Other animals go about the world as nature made them. Why, then, did man start to adorn himself by hanging things round his neck, arms, waist and legs, or putting things on his head? We can imagine many reasons. If an exceptionally strong or brave man succeeded in killing an exceptionally large bear, might he not get the idea of boring a hole through one of its teeth with a sharp flint, and tying the tooth round his neck in order to remind himself of his great achievement, and to show his friends what a great man he was? Gradually it might become the custom in that tribe for all strong and brave hunters to wear a bear's tooth, and it might be regarded as a disgrace not to wear one, and a sign that one was weak or very young.

Another man might make an ornament of a coloured shell or stone simply because he liked it or because its shape reminded him of something. Then if he happened to escape from some danger when he was wearing it he might think the ornament had something to do with it—that it had magic qualities. And his friends and relations would not be satisfied until they had an ornament of the same kind.

People who wore ornaments would soon learn to arrange them in different ways according to their size and colour in order to make them more decorative and impressive. A necklace found in Italy with the skeleton of a young man of the Stone Age was quite elaborate. It consisted of stag's teeth arranged at intervals with, between them, two upper rows made up of the vertebrae of a fish, and one row of shells.

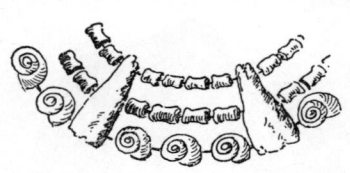

Part of a prehistoric necklace of bones and shells

Another reason why men might tie feathers, horns, skins and all kinds of other things to themselves would be in order to make themselves look fiercer and more terrifying to animals, or to the men of other tribes.

Objects that came from a distance and were therefore scarce —such as sea-shells to people living far inland—would come in time to have a special value, and might be worn only by chiefs and their families, in order to show that they were particularly important people.

Primitive tribes living to-day often associate themselves with some particular animal or bird, such as an eagle or lion, or with a particular place, such as a mountain or river. Man may have started doing this kind of thing very early in his history. Then every member of a group or family may have worn something, such as feathers, claws, or even a stone or wooden object of a certain shape or colour, to represent the animal or mountain or whatever it might be that they believed themselves to be connected with.

So, as we have seen, clothing may have started as ornament, or to distinguish one tribe from another, or to show rank, or because certain things were believed to have magic qualities. But in some places a time came when men and women began to wear clothes for other reasons. During the Ice Ages, when the polar ice spread over far more of the world than it does to-day, some of the districts in which human beings were living became very cold and bleak indeed. Man must have learnt that he would be more comfortable, and more likely to survive, if he covered his body with the skins of animals. At first, perhaps,

he would simply tie a skin round his waist or over his shoulders, but as time passed he would learn how to treat skins in order to make them softer and more supple, and how to join them together in order to make better garments.

A flint scraper

Flint tools have been found buried deep under the earth floors of caves in which prehistoric men sheltered when the weather became colder. Some of the tools were probably used to scrape the inner sides of skins to make them clean, and to hammer the skins in order to make them soft. Stone Age people may also have softened skins in the same way that Eskimo women do to-day, by chewing them. The teeth of Eskimo women are often worn down to stumps by the constant chewing of seal skins.

Among the wonderful flint and bone tools and implements that later cave men made have been found some beautiful bone needles, some not much bigger than those we use to-day. Although the people who made them had only flint tools to work with, some of the needles are finer and more beautifully shaped than those of the Bronze Age, many thousands of years later, or even than those of Roman times.

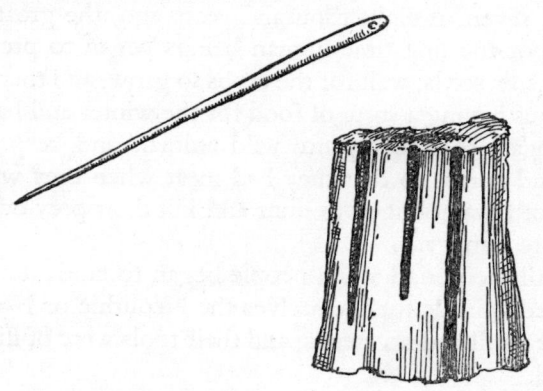

A bone from which splinters have been cut to make needles

Such needles must have been used for sewing skins together in order to make clothes and other coverings, and perhaps also to make bags that would hold water. Possibly the sinews of reindeer and other animals were used as thread.

Bone and ivory pins have been found, too, which were perhaps used to keep the clothes in position. Bones sharpened at one end have been found near the heads of skeletons in Stone Age graves, as though they might have been used to hold the hair in place—in which case they were the first hairpins.

CHAPTER 2

Man Learns How to Make Fabrics

For thousands of years human beings lived by hunting wild animals and by gathering such foods as they could find, and they lived in the open or in caves. The clothes they wore, when they wore any at all, were made from the skins of animals.

Then, seven or eight thousand years ago, the great change began. For the first time human beings began to prepare the ground, sow seeds, wait for the crops to grow, and then harvest them, thus having a store of food for the winter and bad times. They began, too, to capture wild animals and keep them in flocks and herds, so that they had meat when they wanted it, instead of being obliged to hunt and kill their prey every time they were hungry.

We call the period when people began to cultivate the land and breed animals for themselves the Neolithic or New Stone Age. Men still had no metals, and their tools were of flint, bone or wood.

When human beings became farmers they began to settle for long periods in one spot instead of being constantly on the move. Then they had time to learn how to do all kinds of things they had not done before, such as building better homes for themselves, and making baskets and clay pots. And one very important thing they learned was how to make cloth.

Human beings probably found out how to interlace branches in order to make huts and fences quite early—perhaps even before they began to grow crops and herd animals. They probably discovered, too, that if they twisted together several grasses, or the stems of creeping plants, they could make a strong cord.

MAN LEARNS HOW TO MAKE FABRICS

No one can say for certain how and when they learnt to combine these two processes and make cloth.

Before anyone can make a piece of cloth he must have a continuous thread, and thread is made by twisting together the fibres of certain plants, or of wool or hair or some such material. The man (or, more likely, the woman) who first found out how to do this satisfactorily had done something very important indeed.

Which fibres were the very first to be used we cannot say. Neolithic women in different parts of the world probably experimented with many different materials and found that some were better than others. In a district where there were sheep or goats, for instance, some woman may have discovered that if she collected a large mass of the wool or hair which they shed she could draw some of it out from the mass with her fingers and twist it together into a thread, and could continue to draw and twist until she had a great length. As she made her thread she had to wind it on to something—say a short stick—so that it would not get tangled, and after winding she would have to fix it somehow, perhaps in a notch at one end of the stick, so that it would not come unwound while she twisted the next length.

She found, too, in time, that the work was easier if she tied her mass of fibres to one end of another longer stick, (which we now call a distaff), the free end of which she could stick into the ground, or tuck under her arm, thus leaving both hands free.

In India and some other districts, cotton grew wild, and was used from very early times for making fabrics. The cotton fibres cover the seeds inside a pod, or boll as it is called. When the boll is ripe it bursts open, and the mass of white down can be picked off. Someone discovered that thread could be made from these fibres just as they could be made from wool or hair.

One of the surprising things about the early history of spinning and weaving is that people learnt quite early to make linen from the flax plant. The fibres used for making the thread are those which run up the whole length of the stem, and it is quite

19

a long and complicated process to separate them from the outer straw and inner pith, which have to be rotted away, and then to prepare the fibres for spinning.

Spinners soon found that they could let the piece of wood on which they wound the thread as they spun it hang loose at the end of the thread, and if they gave it a twist and set it revolving it would continue to revolve for some time and would itself twist the fibres as the woman drew them out from the mass. They also discovered that if they attached a stone or other weight to the piece of wood on which they wound the thread —the spindle, as we call it—it would twist more evenly and for

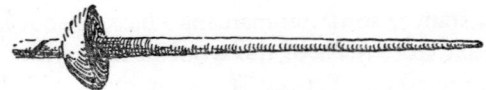

A spindle and whorl

a longer time. We call the weight the 'spindle whorl'. It is usually circular with a hole through the middle, through which the spindle is pushed. When spindle whorls are found in pre-historic settlements we know for certain that the people knew how to spin.

In order to make cloth the thread has to be woven—which means that threads have to be arranged at right angles to other threads and interlaced, much as we darn a hole in a stocking. A weaving loom is simply a frame which holds the first set of threads (the warp) straight and firm while the second set (the weft) are threaded under and over them. It is possible to weave a narrow strip of material without a loom at all, simply by fastening one end of the warp threads to a branch, or something similar, sitting on the ground a few feet away, holding the other ends of the threads, possibly attached to a stick, and passing the weft thread backwards and forwards through them. Some native races still weave in this way, as the earliest weavers of all probably did too.

Weavers soon learnt that it was more satisfactory to set up a framework, or loom. The earliest, simplest form of loom probably consisted of two posts supporting a rod to which the warp threads were fastened. Weights were attached to the bottoms of the warp threads, just above the ground, to keep them taut.

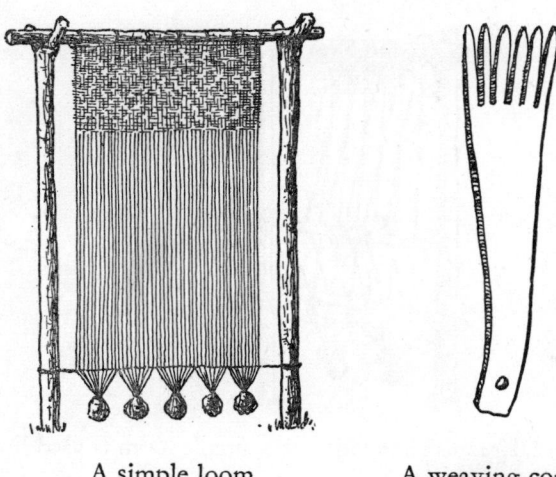

A simple loom   A weaving comb

The weaver stood in front of the loom and lifted up alternate threads with one hand, while she passed the spindle on which the weft thread was wound through with the other. Then she pressed the weft threads close up to each other with a kind of comb.

In time the weaver found ways of making her work easier. She arranged two pairs of supports on the upright posts, and on the lower pair she rested a stick (which we now call the shed stick) which passed through the warp threads, under one and over the next. This made a space between the threads, a 'shed' as it is called—through which she could pass, or throw, her spindle in one direction. But when she wanted to take it back she had to think out a way of bringing forward the threads that had been behind. She did this by resting a second stick (which we now call a heddle-rod) on the other pair of supports on her frame. Each of the threads that lay behind the shed stick she passed through a loop of thread which she attached to the heddle-rod. Then when she wanted to bring these threads forward all she had to do was pull the heddle-rod forward and pass her spindle back through the space formed.

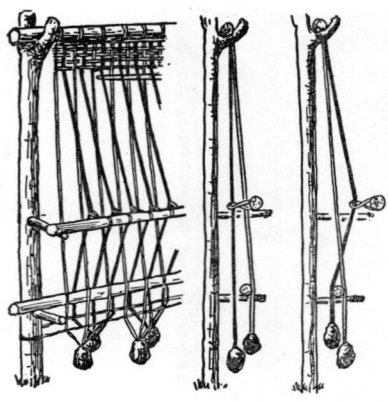

Diagrams showing how a simple loom is used

Of course, the weaving you have just read about is of the very simplest, and in time men and women learnt how to weave complicated patterns. They learnt, too, to dye their yarn and their cloth all kinds of colours by steeping them in liquids in which various natural objects had been boiled. The stems of a plant called indigo, for instance, made a blue dye.

There are other ways of making cloth besides spinning fibres into thread and weaving the thread into a fabric. People who had wool to deal with may have used one of these other methods —felting—even before they learned to spin and weave. Felt is made by wetting, compressing and shrinking wool until it becomes an even smooth material. Some people believe that felt may have been the very first cloth ever made by man.

Whether that is so or not, men probably learnt very early that they could make their woven woollen cloth much closer and warmer by 'fulling' it, as we now call it. This was done for centuries by beating or hammering the wet fabric with a stone or wood block, so that the weft and warp threads were pressed together and the material became closer and thicker, with no spaces between the threads.

Neolithic man in some parts of the world may have learnt how to make cloth from the inner bark of certain trees. Such cloth is still used by people in Polynesia, Africa and South America. The tree, which is often a smallish one belonging to the mulberry family, is cut down, the bark is stripped off, and the inner bark separated and soaked in water. Then the strip of inner bark is beaten with a wooden mallet, and in half an hour the strip has become a square about a yard wide. Other squares are joined on to it, until there is a strip twenty to twenty-five yards long. The material looks something like very tough paper. The people decorate it by pressing pieces of wood against it on which figures in relief have been carved, and which have been damped with coloured dyes. Or they draw lines on it with a comb dipped in colour.

But felt could only be made by people who had wool, and bark cloth could only be made in places where the right kind of trees grew. Spinning and weaving, however, could be done wherever any suitable fibres—wool, flax, cotton, hemp, or whatever it might be—could be found, and the knowledge of how to do it gradually spread north, south, east and west.

When a Stone Age woman had woven a length of cloth she probably tied the ends of the warp threads in twos and threes as she cut them off the loom, so that the cloth would not unravel. So the piece of cloth, which she held in her hands at last, had a fringe at each end.

What would she do with the cloth then? Well, she might wrap her baby in it, or spread it over her children when they were going to sleep, or place it round her own or her husband's shoulders like a shawl, or wrap it round her body and keep it in position with a girdle round her waist—or do any one of many other things. But one thing she certainly would *not* do with it. She would not treat it as we treat a piece of cloth—cut it into odd-shaped pieces and then join the pieces together again. It would not occur to her to attempt to make woven fabric into a garment that would fit the human body closely.

MAN LEARNS HOW TO MAKE FABRICS

For hundreds of years men and women almost everywhere, if they made fabrics at all, used them to wrap or drape around themselves, and if they shaped them at all it was only very little and very simply. The wrapping or draping was done differently in different places, and, as we shall see presently, the people of any one particular country might continue to drape their fabrics in a particular way for hundreds or even thousands of years.

When men made clothes from the skins of animals (as, of course, they continued to do even after they could spin and weave) then the position was rather different. Skins had to be joined together, either because one skin was not large enough by itself, or because the skins were an awkward shape, or because there were torn, damaged pieces which had to be cut away. And because skins are more bulky than fabrics it would be natural to avoid using more than was necessary. So in making a garment from skins, people might try to make it roughly the shape of the person who was going to wear it.

The first more or less fitted jackets and breeches, therefore, were probably made from skins, and it was not until centuries later that people attempted to copy them in fabrics. People who used skins very much discovered that they were improved and made stronger if, after they had been scraped clean and freed from hair, they were soaked in a liquid in which certain plants, or the barks of certain trees, had been soaked. We call this process 'tanning', and the tanned skin we call leather.

CHAPTER 3

Clothes in Ancient Egypt

We talk about the Neolithic or New Stone Age, when men first became farmers; the Bronze Age, when they first began to use metals; the Iron Age, when iron began to replace bronze; but it is very important to remember that men did not reach the same state of development all over the world at the same time. In some places men became skilled farmers thousands of years before they did in others, and men in some districts were using metals for making their tools and weapons many centuries before men in other countries knew that metals existed.

Even to-day there are people living in remote places who are still in the Old Stone Age, and who do not keep flocks and herds, or grow crops or weave fabrics.

Great civilizations were arising in countries bordering the Mediterranean, and in the lands through which the rivers Tigris and Euphrates run, and in the Far East, at a time when the people of northern Europe and of Britain were still living very primitive lives.

Thousands of years ago, when in Britain men still sheltered in caves or in huts made of plaited branches, the people of Ancient Egypt were building great palaces, temples and cities. They were carving statues, too, and painting pictures on the walls of their buildings which give us a very good idea of the kind of clothes they wore and the way they lived. They also wrote books and carved inscriptions in picture-writing at a time when no one in northern Europe could write at all. The Egyptian writings tell us a great deal about their wonderful civilization and their way of life.

CLOTHES IN ANCIENT EGYPT

Ancient Egyptians wore garments made of wool, linen and, later, cotton. From drawings which show men and women spinning and weaving we know that they used the very simplest type of loom, and that their thread was spun by hand with a spindle in the way you have just read about. They did not use a distaff until after Roman times. Yet they produced linen so exquisitely fine and delicate that pieces which have survived from very early times fill present-day experts with amazement. They are finer than our very finest cambric handkerchiefs.

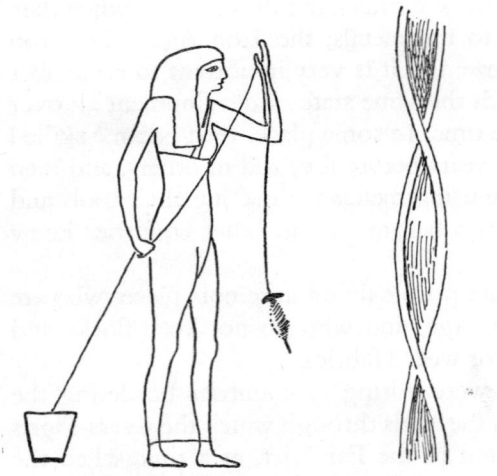
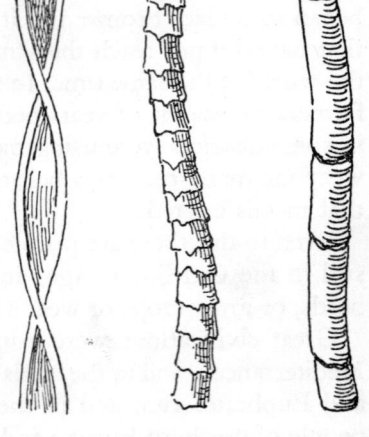

Egyptian woman spinning   Fibres of cotton, wool and linen

The Ancient Egyptians preserved the bodies of people who had died, and wrapped them in strips of linen before putting them in painted wood or stone coffins, which they placed in tombs. When, thousands of years later, some of the tombs were found and modern men examined the 'mummies', as the embalmed bodies are called, they thought at first that the wrappings were of cotton. But when scientists examined the threads through magnifying glasses they found that they were always of linen.

26

CLOTHES IN ANCIENT EGYPT

All fibres have characteristics which enable experts to distinguish them from one another when they see them magnified. Linen fibres are cylindrical and transparent, and are jointed, like pieces of cane or bamboo. Cotton fibres are flat, like narrow pieces of ribbon with a hem or border at the edges, and they twist on themselves slightly to form a spiral. Wool fibres have tiny scales all the way up them which give them a kind of roughness, something like the trunk of a tree.

There are Egyptian drawings which show men harvesting flax (from which linen is made) and preparing it for the spinners. The same treatment is necessary now as was necessary then, thousands of years ago, although now we have all kinds of machines to help us to do the work. In the Egyptian pictures men are shown pulling (not cutting) the flax and tying it into bundles. Then they are shown putting the bundles in tanks in the sun, with weights on them to keep them down under the water. When the outer covering over the fibres began to separate, the bundles of flax were taken out of the water and spread out in the sun to dry. Then the workers spread the flax on flat stones and beat it with wooden mallets to separate the fibres from the outer straw. Afterwards the fibres had to be combed to clean them and to separate the poorer, shorter fibres from the longer, better ones.

After the fibres had been spun into thread and woven into linen cloth, the fabric had to be smoothed, and the Egyptian drawings show men passing wooden rods backwards and forwards over it. Wooden planes, something the shape of our irons, have been found which were probably used for smoothing linen after it had been washed.

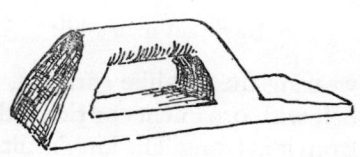

A wooden plane found in Egypt, probably used for smoothing linen

Immense quantities of flax must have been grown in Ancient Egypt, for besides using linen for their own garments, and for wrapping the bodies of their dead, the Egyptians exported at great deal to other countries. The 'fine linen' of Egypt was famous by the time written records came to be made, and it is often mentioned in the Bible.

The drawings and sculptures of Egypt show us the shapes of the clothes worn by Egyptian men and women, but we have to use a little imagination if we are to form any idea of what they really looked like. For thousands of years Egyptian artists represented human beings and the clothes they wore in very much the same way. They made no attempt to make draperies look soft and natural, and robes made of the finest, lightest material are drawn or carved as though they were cut out of something stiff and hard.

Workmen and servants are generally shown in Egyptian pictures wearing nothing but a loin cloth or else a kind of skirt or kilt, very short, which crosses over in front and is held in place by a girdle that also ties in front. Upper-class men are shown

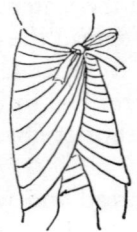 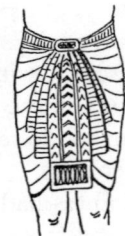

Egyptian man's kilt   Kilt with ornamental belt

wearing the kilt-like garment, too, but often with an elaborate belt with ornaments or richly decorated material hanging down from it in front. The king's kilt, or apron, was decorated in front with lions' heads, and a border of asps, or serpents (which were the symbol of royalty) was embroidered round it, and sometimes the king's name. The lions' heads and other decorations of the same kind may perhaps have been cut out of coloured leather.

Over the kilt men of the upper classes usually wore a wide full garment of fine linen or cotton. It was made by taking a strip of material about one and a quarter yards wide and twice the height of the wearer in length and folding it over in the centre. Then a round hole was cut for the neck, and the front of the garment was slit down a little way so that there was room for the head to go through. Then the two sides were sewn together nearly to the top, where an opening was left big enough for the arms to go through. The robe might be worn loose, or a belt or girdle might be worn round the waist.

You will find that this kind of robe turns up again and again in different countries, but treated in many different ways.

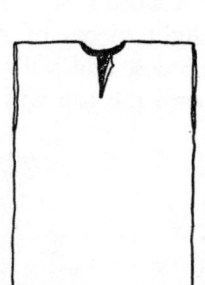

Diagram of an Egyptian sleeveless robe

Egyptian wearing a robe and sash

Sometimes the Egyptian robe was not sewn up at the sides at all. Then, after it had been put over the head, the front half was wrapped around the body and fastened at the waist at the back, and the back half was wrapped round to the front. Then a long sash, eighteen inches or more wide, was wrapped twice round the body and tucked in in front.

Another type of garment which was worn in Ancient Egypt we shall meet again and again in different forms for centuries, since it has been worn from the very earliest times even to the present day. It is the very simplest kind of tunic, made, like the robe, by folding a piece of material across the centre and cutting out a hole for the neck. Then instead of simply joining up the sides and leaving holes for the arms to go through, two pieces are cut away, one on each side, from below the arm to the bottom of the garment. When the side seams have been stitched up, a T-shaped tunic is the result, the same shape as a modern man's short-sleeved vest. As we shall see, the T-shaped tunic can be long or short, wide or narrow. The Egyptian tunic was generally long enough to reach the ankles.

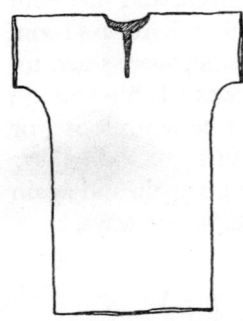

Diagram of a T-shaped tunic

Women often wore a skirt made of two wide straight pieces of material joined up the sides, and with a cord threaded through the top which they tied in front to keep the skirt in place. Sometimes the skirt had no waist cord, but the wearer, after putting the skirt on, took two pieces of the upper edge, about half a yard apart, in her hands, twisted them into a kind of cord and knotted them in front.

Very often women wore no upper garment, but sometimes they took a strip of material about two feet wide and placed it round their shoulders, tying the two front corners together. Or they might take a long, wide rectangle of material and place one of the narrower ends round their necks, knotting the two front corners at the waist and so forming a long, loose cloak.

Egyptian clothes were nearly always drawn close to the body and legs at the back and any fulness was brought to the front. The fabrics used were so fine

Egyptian woman wearing a skirt, cape, wide collar and head-dress

30

that they were transparent, so that the body and limbs of the wearer showed through.

Some Egyptians, both men and women, instead of wearing wide, full garments, wore narrow, close-fitting ones. One often shown in the drawings reached from just below the breast to the ankles and was held in place by straps over the shoulders. Other Egyptians sometimes dressed themselves by draping a strip of material about five yards long around their bodies and over their shoulders very much as present-day Indian women do when they wear the garment we call a sari.

All Egyptian garments were very simple in shape, but the materials were often dyed gay colours, or had patterns woven into them or printed on them. Egypt was famous for embroidery, too, and there are references in the Old Testament to 'fine linen with broidered work from Egypt'. Sometimes plain materials had coloured borders, and they were fringed at the ends. Both men and women wore many elaborate ornaments such as gold ear-rings, bangles, necklaces and finger rings set with precious stones. They were fond, too, of beads made of glazed pottery, faience beads as we call them, which were generally blue. Nearly all upper-class Egyptians wore wide, flat necklaces, like round collars.

Egyptian priests wore clothes similar to those worn by other men, but in the temple they were not allowed to wear anything but linen. In later times they seem to have been allowed to wear cotton garments outside the temple. The Rosetta stone, which we can see in the British Museum, has an inscription on it written in three different scripts, one in Greek and the others in two different kinds of Egyptian writing. It was probably written about 196 B.C. and it mentions cotton garments supplied for the use of the priests. They were allowed, too, to wear an outer cloak made of wool, but they had to take it off before entering the temple, and they must not at any time wear a woollen garment that touched the skin. The Egyptians believed that a fabric woven from fibres that came from an animal was not so clean as one made from fibres that came from a plant. That is why linen only was used for wrapping the bodies of the dead.

The Chief Priest wore a leopard skin over his linen robes when he was officiating in the temple. This may have been a survival from very early forgotten times, before the Egyptians used woven fabrics very much. We often find that the clothes worn by men taking part in religious ceremonies are those of a previous age, and the gods in many countries are represented wearing clothes that were fashionable hundreds, or even thousands, of years earlier than the time at which the pictures of them were painted or the statues carved.

All Egyptian men shaved their heads and faces and those of the upper classes wore wigs of curled and plaited hair indoors and out. Even small boys had their heads shaved, but certain locks were left at the sides. Princes, when they grew up, wore a badge or emblem at the side of their wigs or head-dresses which hung down to the shoulder and represented this lock of hair. It indicated their rank. On state occasions the king wore a double crown, to show that he was king of both lower and upper Egypt.

The Egyptians seem to have had a great contempt for people who did not shave, and to have regarded bearded men as slovenly and dirty. They themselves only allowed their hair and beards to grow when they were in mourning. And yet an odd thing is that they sometimes wore false beards tied under their chins. Ordinary men had a little short beard about two inches long, but the king wore a long one cut square at the bottom. The gods were represented with beards that turned up at the bottom, and when a king had died and his people believed that he had joined the gods they sometimes placed a turned-up beard on his statue.

Workmen and lower servants did not wear wigs, but either close caps or nothing at all on their heads, although they too usually shaved off all their hair. The Greek writer Herodotus, who was the world's first great historian, declared that Egyptian skulls, which he had seen on a battlefield, were exceptionally hard and thick. He said it was because the Egyptians shaved their heads from early youth and exposed them to the sun without any covering.

An Egyptian wig

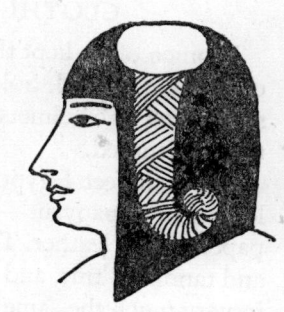

An Egyptian prince

The crowns of upper and lower
Egypt

An Egyptian Royal
head-dress

False beards worn
by men, kings, and
gods

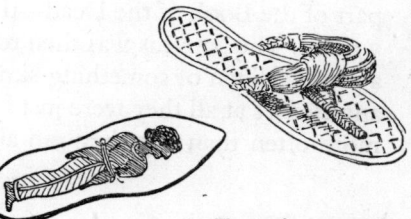

Egyptian sandals

c

Women often kept their own hair and had it very elaborately curled and plaited. Soldiers wore thickly padded, quilted caps, something like helmets, with a point at the top from which two tassels dangled.

On their feet Egyptians wore sandals made of plaited palm leaves, or of papyrus—the reed from which they made a kind of paper—or of leather. Their drawings show Egyptians preparing and tanning skins, and making sandals and other leather goods, in very much the same way as these things have been done ever since, until the invention of machinery.

Egyptian sandal-maker at work

An Egyptian sometimes had his enemy's portrait painted on the sole of his own sandal, so that he should tread him underfoot at every step.

But Egyptians often went barefooted, and in any case they took off their sandals when they entered a temple or a friend's house.

They liked carrying and wearing flowers, and pictures show guests being presented with a lotus flower to hold, and having necklaces of flowers put round their necks and on their head. Servants replaced the garlands as they began to fade.

Sometimes the Egyptians wore charms which they thought would ward off disease, or would cure an illness if they had one. And they often hung a string of beads round a child's neck with a charm hanging from it which was supposed to make the child grow up wise and virtuous, and to protect him from evil. The charm was often in the form of a piece of papyrus on which part of the Book of the Dead—the Egyptian sacred book—was written. The papyrus was then rolled up tightly and sewn up in a piece of linen or something similar. If children in Egypt wore any clothes at all they were just like those of their parents, but more often than not they ran about naked.

CHAPTER 4

Old Testament Times

We have seen how the people of Ancient Egypt dressed. What kind of clothes did the people of other nations we read about in the Old Testament wear—the people who lived north and east of Egypt, in the lands we call Mesopotamia and Persia?

In these lands, as in Egypt, archaeologists have excavated the ancient cities of the Sumerians, Babylonians, Assyrians and Persians, each of whose great empires flourished and declined, conquered and were in their turn overwhelmed, during the two or three thousand years before the birth of Christ. They have found pictures and statues, seals and coins which give us some idea what the inhabitants of these countries looked like in the days of their greatness.

Some of the very earliest statues represent men who lived about three thousand years before Christ. They are shown with shaven heads and upper lips, but with a fringe of beard round their chins from ear to ear, very much like those worn by Englishmen about a hundred years ago. They are wearing short skirt-like garments from the waist to below the knee, which look as if they are made of overlapping leaves or petals. But this is believed to be

Soldier and king—3000 B.C.

35

the artist's way of representing the loosely hanging wool on the outside of a sheepskin. Other very early sculptures and pictures show men wearing hoods with a point on top, which were probably made by folding a rectangle of fur in half and sewing up one side.

Slightly later sculptures show men wearing clothing that was certainly made from woven fabrics. But again we have to use our imaginations and put in the folds and fulnesses which the ancient artist has left out. When we examine the costumes carefully, or if we try to clothe a present-day person in the same way, we find that, as in Egypt, fabrics were cut and shaped very little, and sometimes not at all. They were simply wrapped and draped round the wearer—but each country had its own method of draping and of dealing with details and decoration.

In the British Museum in London there is a statue of an Sumerian king named Gudea who lived about 2500 B.C. He is draped in a piece of cloth which must have been about ten feet long and four and a half feet wide. It is wrapped twice round his body, just under the armpits, then thrown over the left shoulder from front to back, and the top corner is brought round under his right arm and tucked in in front. With this kind of draping the left arm and shoulder were completely covered unless the wearer raised his arm, while the right arm and shoulder were bare, for the king does not appear to have worn any other garment.

The head-dress worn by a Sumerian queen who lived about the

King Gudea—2500 B.C.

36

same time as Gudea has been found in her tomb. It is made up of gold ribbons, leaves and rosettes and has some of the blue stones which we call lapis lazuli set in the gold. Seven long thin stems of gold, with a gold rosette on the tip of each, stand up at the back, and a fringe of gold rings in front would have hung over the queen's forehead.

Assyrian about 1000 B.C.   An Assyrian hunter

Shawls similar to Gudea's were worn for centuries, but by Assyrian times (13th to 6th centuries B.C.) men more often wore a short-sleeved, fairly close-fitting T-shaped tunic which varied in length. Sometimes the men placed a kind of apron over the tunic (but worn at the back instead of in front) and nearly always they are shown with a close-fitting belt about ten inches wide, and probably of leather, round the waist, with a little narrow belt over it. Sometimes they are shown wearing the big shawl over the tunic, and sometimes they have a fringed strip of material wrapped round the waist and then thrown over one shoulder and hanging down the back.

A head-dress found in a queen's tomb. About 2500 B.C.

King Assur-nasir-pal, ninth century B.C.

Assyrian head-dresses

King Assur-nasir-pal, who lived in the ninth century B.C., is shown wearing the usual tunic, but over it a wide rectangular shawl has been put on in this way. A piece of material about two and a half yards long by two yards wide, with a fringe along the two longer sides, was folded along its length so that there were two tiers of fringe visible, one about eighteen inches or so above the other. A cord was attached at one end of the fold. The wearer draped the shawl by holding the cord at his waist on the right side with the shawl passing over the right shoulder and hanging down the back. Then he brought the fold across the back of his neck, down loosely over his left shoulder and arm, making a kind of pouch for the left arm to rest in, across the front, round the waist, under the right arm, across the back and round to the front again. About six inches in front of the waist on the left side he folded what was left of the shawl under, and placed a cord round the waist to hold the whole thing in position. Finally he tied the first cord, which was hanging forward from his right shoulder, on to the waist cord.

A queen is shown wearing the same kind of draped shawl over her tunic. Women generally seem to have worn a narrow, straight tunic like those of the men, but without the belt. Sometimes they wore a short cape round their shoulders. Their hair was very elaborately dressed, and their heads were decorated with gold ornaments or bound with twisted fabrics.

The Assyrians were very fond of fringes and tassels, and put them everywhere possible. And, although their clothes were so simple in shape, they were very lavishly decorated with embroidered patterns and were stiff with gold and jewels, so that hardly an inch of plain material remained. Both men and women wore armlets and ear-rings and, sometimes, high round collars round their necks as well as rings on their fingers and crowns on their heads.

The Assyrians and Babylonians wore their bushy black hair down to their shoulders. It was curled and waved, and so were their square-cut beards. Often they wore a fillet of material or of metal round their heads, and they are very frequently shown wearing a round hat, something like the fez that used to be worn in Turkey, though the Assyrian hat had no tail or tassel. Kings and gods are shown wearing a higher fez, with a point on top and a strip of material round the lower edge which finished with two ribbons hanging down the back with fringes at the ends. Or they wore a tall domed turban. They wore san-

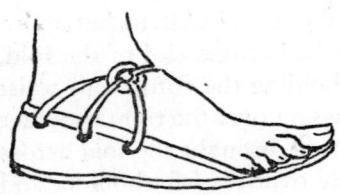

An Assyrian sandal

dals on their feet, or were bare-footed, and for hunting and fighting they wore soft leather boots.

The Persians, too, wore their own shoulder-length hair and had beards and moustaches, though sometimes their heads, necks and chins (especially those of servants and soldiers) were entirely covered by a hood. Their beards were round or pointed, not square like those of the Assyrians. Round their heads, low down on the forehead, they sometimes wore a fillet of twisted cloth, or else they wore round hats, or head-dresses shaped like crowns. The king wore a crown of this kind which was six or eight inches high and wider at the top than at the base.

Darius of Persia (who lived in the sixth and fifth centuries B.C.) is shown wearing a robe something like those worn by the Egyptians, but arranged differently. It has been made from a length of material twice his height, folded over and with a hole cut in the centre for his head to go through. Then the sides have been sewn up, but about twenty inches has been left on both sides for armholes. Then a tight belt or girdle has been fastened round the waist, and the sides of the robe have been drawn up over it in big pouches.

Persian head-dresses

Often Persians are shown wearing the usual T-shaped tunic, knee-length, but unlike those of the Egyptians and Assyrians, the Persian tunic often had sleeves to the wrist.

Persian women seem to have worn long, straight, rather narrow tunics, sometimes with shawls or fringed strips of fabric draped over them—very much as the Assyrian women did.

But there is something that makes the costumes of Ancient Persia particularly interesting to us. That is that for the first time people are shown wearing *coats* and *trousers*. One coat is very like the T-shaped tunic, but is open right down the front.

Darius of Persia   Persians in coats and trousers

It has a fringe all round it, and a chain or cord linking the two edges. Another coat is much more modern in shape, for it has a sewn-in sleeve, a flat, turned-down collar, and cuffs, and the man wearing it has long trousers drawn in rather tightly at the ankles. The trousers may have been made of leather. A Greek writer named Xenophon tells us that the Persians wore gloves on their hands in winter.

So the clothes worn by Persian men were, in many ways, very like those worn centuries later in western Europe.

Many of the characters whose names are mentioned in the Old Testament were dressed in some such way as the people we have been reading about. But what about the Hebrews themselves?

Most of the famous pictures illustrating Bible stories which we can see in picture galleries and ancient churches were painted far away in western Europe many hundreds of years after the events took place. The characters are shown wearing either the clothes of the painter's own time, or those which had become especially associated with that particular character, though they may not have been the kind of clothes he or she actually wore when alive.

Hebrews sometimes appear in ancient Egyptian pictures and sculptures, but as captives or slaves. Palestine lay on the main route connecting the two great areas of civilization in pre-Christian times—the Nile valley and the valleys of the Tigris and the Euphrates—so that she was liable to be dominated by whichever nation happened to be most powerful and triumphant at any one time, Egypt, Assyria, Babylon, Persia or, later, Greece and Rome. In their dress and in their customs the Hebrews were influenced by their powerful neighbours and conquerors.

When we first hear of the Hebrews they were wandering shepherds, driving their flocks and herds from place to place over the desert in search of good pastures, and living in tents. Their first great leader, Abraham, who, the Bible tells us, was born at a town called Ur on the Euphrates, led his tribe westwards into Canaan, then south into Egypt for a time, then back to Canaan, where they settled. These events took place probably between two and three thousand years before the birth of Christ.

Abraham quite possibly wore a large fringed shawl such as King Gudea wore, and it was almost certainly made of a woollen fabric. In the winter he and his family probably kept themselves warm with sheepskins and other furs. They probably protected their heads and necks from the sun and driving sand in summer just as present-day Arabs do, by arranging a cloth over their heads and holding it in place with a twisted cloth or cord. Ancient sculptures, too, sometimes show Hebrew captives wearing a pointed cap, as a great many ancient races seem to have done, and a relief found at Nineveh, the capital city of Assyria, shows quite clearly that the caps sometimes had ear flaps that could be turned back over the head.

From the Canaanites, in whose land they settled, the Hebrews seem to have adopted the custom of weaving their fabrics in coloured stripes, some wide and some narrow, and this kind of material became characteristic of them. Possibly the 'coat of many colours' which Joseph's father made for him, and which made his brothers so jealous that they sold him into slavery, may have been a kind of tunic made of this gaily striped fabric.

Of course, the Hebrews also wore garments of plain colours, one garment of one colour over another of a different colour, or a striped garment over a plain one.

You remember that the Bible tells us how Joseph's father and brothers and their families followed him to Egypt and settled there, and how their descendants were oppressed and enslaved by the Egyptians until Moses led them forth again and back to the 'Promised Land' of Canaan.

Moses, who had been brought up at Pharaoh's Court, probably wore, in Egypt, the same clothes as those worn by well-to-do Egyptians. The other Hebrews, when they appear in ancient Egyptian pictures, wear the scanty clothes worn by the poorest slaves and servants. But during their long bondage they probably learnt something of the Egyptians' skill in embroidery. We read in the Bible that after leaving Egypt they were ordered by God to build a tabernacle, and they told to make a hanging for the door of 'blue and purple and scarlet and fine twined linen, wrought with needle work'.

They made an embroidered coat for Aaron the Priest, too. The Egyptians had learnt very early how to make thread from pure gold, and we read that the Israelites, when they made a garment called an ephod for Aaron to wear when he was conducting services in the temple, 'did beat the gold into thin plates, and cut it into wires to work it in the blue and in the purple and in the scarlet and in the fine linen, with cunning work'.

By this time, probably, Hebrew men were wearing short-

A Hebrew

sleeved T-shaped tunics, fringed round the bottom and reaching to the ankles, with the shawl described above draped over it. But as time went on some of them took to wearing two tunics, the under one of linen with close-fitting long sleeves and the upper one of wool. The upper one then had very wide elbow-length sleeves.

Sometimes over the linen under-tunic men wore a kind of plain T-shaped coat, open down the front, something like the Persian one, but with no collar and with the sleeves reaching only to the elbow.

Another coat-like garment, open up the front, was wide and straight, with no sleeves but with openings in the side seams for the arms to go through. It was very like the Egyptian and other robes we have read about, except for being open in front. Often the sides were not joined either, but were held together by cords from one to the other.

Over their under-tunics the Hebrews wore a wide belt, something like those worn by the Assyrians. In early times the belt was of leather, but later it was often of richly embroidered or woven or striped fabric, sometimes set with jewels. The garments worn over the tunic were unbelted and hung very loose and full.

The edges of the coat-like garments, like the bottom of the tunic, were trimmed with fringes, for in their scriptures the Hebrews read that God had said to Moses, 'Speak unto the children of Israel and bid them that they make them fringes in the borders of their garments throughout the generations, and that they put upon the fringes of the borders a ribband of blue.'

At each corner of the coats or shawls the Hebrews sewed a purple tassel, the tassels standing for the four consonants of the name Jehovah.

Hebrew women, at first, wore a very simple dress, just a long, straight, almost sleeveless tunic to the ankles, with a girdle. Later on women wore a robe like the man's, with long, open sleeves and without a girdle, or with, perhaps, a striped sash round the hips. Sometimes they wore a sleeveless coat, like the man's, over it. Their clothes gradually became very loose and much more voluminous.

Like the women of Assyria, they dressed their hair very elaborately and decorated their heads with dangling gold ornaments and sequins. Often they wore close-fitting caps, low on the forehead, with little gold discs all round the edge and over the top. Over it they wore a veil of thin white material, or a large scarf with an embroidered edge. In the temple they had to wear a transparent veil which covered the whole head and face.

They wore gold ornaments on their arms and necks, and some of them took a great deal of interest in their clothes, which annoyed serious, thoughtful people very much. The Bible speaks of the tinkling ornaments about their feet, and of their chains and bracelets, their head-bands and ear-rings, their fine linen, their many robes, mantles and veils, and tells them that the Lord will punish them for wearing all this finery. But, as we shall see, all through the ages fine clothes, jewels and unusual garments have been criticized and people, both men and women, have been threatened with all kinds of terrible penalties for wearing them.

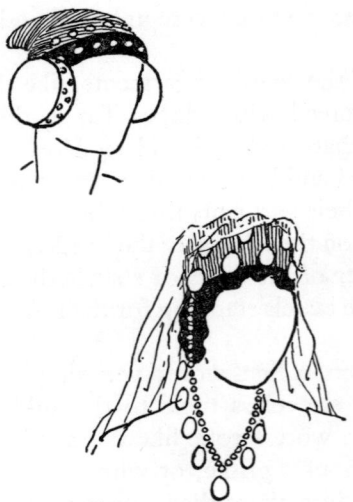

Hebrew women's head-dresses

CHAPTER 5

In Crete and Ancient Greece

If anyone had asked an archaeologist a hundred years ago how the peoples of the ancient pre-Christian civilizations dressed, he would have answered that they all wore draped, straight, or very simply shaped garments such as you have been reading about up to now.

But since the 1870s archaeologists have been excavating on the island of Crete at the eastern end of the Mediterranean, and in the neighbourhood of Mycenae and Tyrens on the Greek mainland, and they have discovered the remains of a wonderful civilization which they did not know before had ever even existed. Stories about it and its heroes had come down to us, but everybody believed that they were just myths or fairy tales.

The excavators found the ruins of great buildings, such as the palace of Minos at Knossos in Crete, and they also found statuettes of Cretan goddesses, vases decorated with representations of human beings and animals, and rooms with pictures painted on the walls which were still clear after more than three thousand years.

One of the astonishing things about the sculptured and painted figures of this ancient Aegean civilization was that their clothes were so different from those of Egypt, Assyria and the rest of the ancient world. Some of the earliest statuettes were found in Crete. They dated from about 3000 B.C., and were of women who appeared to be clothed in dresses of which the skirts stood out like the crinolines of Victorian days, while at the back of the neck was a stiff upstanding collar. Even more surprising, women's dresses of a thousand or so years later were covered from waist to hem with narrow frills or flounces, and the bodices were tight-fitting, with tiny waists.

The earlier type of dress may have been made of leather or else of thick wool cloth made by felting the wool instead of spinning it into thread and weaving it. You can find out what the dress looked like by clothing a small doll or puppet. Take a

Minoan woman of
about 3000 B.C.

Minoan snake-goddess,
about 2000 B.C.

piece of felt or very stiff cloth, or even paper, cut it into a semi-circle with the straight edge about twice the length of the doll from shoulder to ground. Make two holes for the arms to go through, a short distance on each side of the centre and about half the doll's chest measurement from the straight edge. Put the garment on the doll and tie a girdle fairly tightly round the waist. You will find that the skirt will form a kind of bell-shape, and that the material at the back of the neck will stand up stiffly.

The women who wore this kind of dress decorated it by sewing strips of a different material, which may have been leather, down the skirt.

The later dresses, with tight bodices, laced across the front, and flounced skirts, are much more elaborate and more difficult to account for. The fitted bodices may, in the beginning, have been made from the skins of animals, since the Cretans were very skilful leather workers and made shields and high boots and many other things of leather. Later the tightly fitted bodices were copied in woven fabrics—though why the Cretans, unlike other people of ancient times, should have done this we do not know.

Even the frills on the skirts are believed by some authorities to be imitations in fabric of sheepskin garments made with the wool left on, on the outside. The wool then hangs down unevenly below the edge of the garment, giving a flounced effect. You read in Chapter 4 about the very ancient statuettes found in Mesopotamia which show men wearing skirts that appear to be made up of overlapping petals, but which we believe were really made from sheepskins with the wool left on.

Round their waists the Cretan women wore tight close-fitting belts, sometimes thick and padded and sometimes of metal and shaped to fit the figure. Sometimes they wore a kind of overskirt over the flounced dress, like a double apron, longer at the back than the front. On their heads they wore tall, three-tier head-dresses, or else round flattish hats, rather the shape of a tam-o'-shanter. Their long hair hung loose, to their waists or below.

Men, too, wore their hair long and flowing. They are often shown without any clothes at all, except a belt into which a dagger is thrust, though sometimes, especially when taking part in some ceremony, they seem to have worn a very short apron in front and a slightly longer one at the back.

For a time, round about 1500 B.C., they seem to have worn a kilt, knee-length, with a tight belt, and occasionally they are shown wearing a deep jewelled collar, rather like the one the Egyptians used to wear.

Women seem to have been athletes and bull-fighters, just as men were. When they are taking part in such sports both sexes

A Minoan woman athlete

are shown in the paintings wearing the short double aprons, the belt, the leather boots, and with their long hair flying. The skins of the women are painted white and those of the men brownish-red, but otherwise there is very little to distinguish them from one another.

As well as these typical clothes, the people of Crete and

Mycenae seem occasionally to have worn the universal T-shaped tunic. This was the same for men and women, though the men's were usually shorter. The tunics seem to have been decorated with strips of contrasting material down the seams and round the neck.

About 1200 B.C. the Aegean civilization was attacked by barbaric invaders and collapsed. The palaces and temples were destroyed and in time forgotten, and the survivors were scattered. We do not know very much about what happened during the next few hundred years.

The flounced skirts, tight-fitting bodices, small waists, aprons and kilts of the Aegeans disappeared with them.

The clothes worn by their successors, the Greeks, some centuries later were quite different.

With the Greeks we have reached the days of written history, of literature and philosophy, of great art and architecture, and of some of the finest sculpture the world has ever known. When we look at Greek statues it is not necessary for us to use our imaginations in order to change stiff, tight, hard-looking garments into the loose, flowing robes we know from their shape and material they must have been. Greek artists were quite capable of representing the folds of drapery in all their beauty and variety, just as they could represent the ideal beauty of the human figure more perfectly than ever before.

Greek clothes were extremely simple and very graceful, and they changed very little in shape during the six hundred years or so before the Greeks came under the domination of the Romans.

The two great branches of the Greek people were called Dorians and Ionians. The chief city of the Dorians was Sparta and that of the Ionians was Athens. Until the sixth century B.C. almost all Greek women wore a robe which we call the Doric chiton (pronounced kyton). It was made of woollen material. In order to see what this kind of dress was like to wear you should get someone to stand with her arms outstretched on either side. Then take a piece of fabric twice as long as her width from elbow to elbow and about eighteen inches wider

The Doric chiton

than her height from shoulder to ground. Fold the eighteen inches over along the whole length of the material; then fold the material again down the centre so that the eighteen inch strip falls on the outside. Place the material round the person you are dressing so that the fold comes on the left side and the two edges on the right. Fasten it on the shoulder, back over front, with two pins, which in Ancient Greece were long dagger-like implements.

In some districts, such as Sparta itself, where they believed in hardening the body and not coddling it, the Doric chiton was worn without a girdle, so that the right side of the body was bare. But more often a girdle was worn round the waist, and sometimes the two edges of the chiton were sewn together. There is a statue of the Goddess Artemis wearing a chiton of this kind in the Athens museum. It is one of the earliest surviving Greek statues.

The Doric chiton varied a little. For instance, sometimes the fold-over at the top was made much wider so that it reached to the hips, and the girdle was tied over it. The goddess Athena was clothed in this kind of chiton in a wonderful ivory and gold statue which a Greek sculptor named Phideas made for the Parthenon in Athens. The statue was very famous indeed. We, of course, only know it from copies. There is a cast of one such copy in the British Museum.

The chiton was not cut to fit the wearer but was woven to the right size on the loom, with a coloured or patterned border at each end (these ends would be the edges at the right side of the wearer) and sometimes with a border all the way round. The borders were sometimes in the form of geometric patterns and sometimes they represented animals or human beings. The same ornaments were used as we find in Greek architecture. Often the whole of the material of which the chiton was made had a pattern woven into it, which was generally geometric, and sometimes patterns were embroidered or printed.

At a place called Kertch in the Crimea some fragments of actual Greek fabrics of the fifth and fourth centuries B.C. were found. Some had woven patterns, some were embroidered; one had a pattern painted on it. One piece was of violet coloured wool, and had the well-known Greek 'palmette' pattern embroidered on it in gold and green.

Greek palmette pattern

More recently some fragments of Greek fabrics, probably dating from the end of the fifth century B.C., were found in a bronze jar near Athens. One was of linen which had been embroidered with an all-over pattern in the form of rectangles containing lions—a pattern rather like those that were popular in Persia at the time. The embroidery was done in silk, but all the silk has vanished. We can still see what the pattern was like because of the holes made in the linen by the needle and thread. You can see these fragments for yourself at the Victoria and Albert Museum in London.

Silk is something we have not mentioned before. The Chinese discovered, perhaps as early as 2500 B.C., that they could unwind the delicate filament from the cocoon which a certain kind of caterpillar made for itself, and from it could make thread and weave beautiful, soft, lustrous fabrics. A Chinese empress of the time was one of the first people to encourage the cultivation of silkworms, and of the mulberry trees on the leaves of which they feed.

For nearly three thousand years after that the Chinese jealously guarded their secret. The lovely silken fabrics found their way to other countries, first to China's near neighbours and later to lands far away in the West. For centuries people outside China could only guess as to how silk was made, and their guesses were generally nowhere near the truth. Embassies were sent to China to try to persuade the Chinese to disclose the secret, but without success.

The Greek philosopher Aristotle, who lived in the fourth century B.C. and was Alexander the Great's tutor, speaks of silk, and says that silk fabrics were woven in the Greek island of Cos. This must have been from raw silk imported from the East. Silk fabrics, whether they had been woven in this way or whether they had made the long journey overland from China, cost more than their weight in gold, so only the very wealthiest could buy them and silk was very rare and precious.

We can be sure that the Doric chitons worn by most Greeks were made of wool, often, probably, spun and woven by women in their own homes. Men as well as women wore the chiton, when they were clothed at all, but the man's chiton was generally only knee length, and was often fastened on the left shoulder only, leaving the right arm and shoulder bare. High, soft boots were often worn by workmen and travellers, though sandals or bare feet were the usual wear at other times.

Herodotus tells us how the Greek women came to abandon the Doric chiton, which had been the national dress, and take to wearing a slightly different chiton called the Ionic. The story, according to Herodotus, is that in the sixth century B.C. a military expedition in which the Athenian army was engaged ended disastrously, and all the Athenian soldiers were put to death except one, who managed to escape and reach Athens with the terrible news. The distressed wives and mothers, enraged by what had happened to their men, and filled with contempt for the one man who had come back, seized the dagger-like pins which fastened their chitons at the shoulders and stabbed the unfortunate man to death.

The governors of Athens were appalled at this barbarism, and declared that from that time onward the women should wear the Ionic chiton which the Greeks living on the coasts of Asia Minor had adopted, so Herodotus tells us, from their neighbours the Carians.

However true or not this story may be it is certainly a fact that from about the sixth century B.C. the Ionic chiton did replace the Doric. The two types of chiton were made in almost exactly the same way. The main difference between them was that the Ionic chiton had no turn-over strip at the top, and it was fastened on the shoulders by a series of brooches at intervals instead of with two long pins. It was placed round the figure just as the Doric chiton was, with the fold on the left of the wearer and the edges on the right. Sometimes the edges were joined, in which case the openings for the hands to go through were nearly always in the top edge, in line with the neck, not in the sides.

A double girdle was often worn over the chiton, especially when it was necessary to make it shorter because the wearer was going to do something active. Sometimes the dress was drawn up over the girdle in a big pouch. At other times a narrow girdle was crossed between the breasts or at the back, taken over the shoulders, and tied round the waist.

The Doric chiton, you remember, was of wool, and therefore warm, but the Ionic was of linen and was often thin and transparent. So in cold weather it was necessary to wear a cloak over it. The Greek cloak was called a himation. It was a rectangular

The Ionic chiton

strip of material, often about twice the length of the wearer from elbow to elbow with arms outstretched, just as the chiton was, and might be wide enough to reach somewhere between the hips and the knees, or wider, so that it reached to the ankles. Often it was placed round the figure in the same way as the chiton was, but was only fastened on one shoulder, on the side of the open edges, the folded side being arranged in pleats under the other arm. The himation, like the chiton, often had a coloured or patterned border.

But the himation varied a great deal both in size and in the way it was arranged. Often it was wrapped round the wearer's body and over the shoulders very much as the large shawls of other countries were. Sometimes it was big enough to cover the whole figure, including the head, and sometimes the upper part

A Greek woman wearing
the himation

A Greek boy wearing
a chlamys

of it was folded over before it was put on, as the Doric chiton was.

Soldiers and horsemen often wore a smaller cloak, about seven feet long by three and a half feet wide, which was called a chlamys. It was worn so that it covered the left arm and shoulder and was fastened on the right shoulder.

IN CRETE AND ANCIENT GREECE

The big, more dignified himation was worn by older men and always by philosophers and thinkers. Often they wore no other garment, and they draped the himation round their waists and hung it over the left arm, leaving the upper part of the body bare. Statues of Sophocles and Demosthenes, in Rome, show them draped in this way. But quite often a chiton was worn under the himation.

Some women were evidently in the habit of wearing several garments one on top of another, and this was considered extravagant. So in 594 B.C. a law was passed ordaining that no woman was to wear more than three garments. This is an early example of a kind of order which, as we shall see, has been issued again and again in country after country in an attempt to make people dress as the government of the time thought they should. Such laws have very seldom had much effect.

After Alexander the Great's expedition against the Persians in the fourth century B.C. some Greeks took to wearing long sleeves, as the Persians did.

In the early days of Greece, youths wore their hair long, but plaited it and twisted it round their heads when they were taking part in athletics or some other energetic activity. A sixth century B.C. sculptured head of the god Zeus shows him with a curled fringe on the forehead, rather like those of the Assyrians, and with the rest of his long hair looped and bound at the back. Some men tied a band round their heads and turned most of their hair up and tucked it into it, just leaving one or two long curls free to hang down on to the shoulders. After about 480 B.C. it became fashionable for young men to cut their hair short, though they still tied a ribbon round their heads, or wore a gold or bronze fillet.

Young boys wore their hair long, but had it cut off when they became men. The long hair was then offered as a sacrifice to the gods.

Women in the early days either let their hair flow freely, or bound it with ribbons and looped it up. But during the latter part of the fourth century B.C. they began to draw it back very simply and arrange it in a knot at the nape of the neck—very

57

much as many women do now if their hair is not cut short. Later on, hair styles became very varied and elaborate with ribbons and nets and bands to confine the hair and hold it in position.

The Greeks often went about barefooted, especially indoors, but they also wore sandals. Men, if they needed more protection for their feet when they were hunting, fighting or riding, wore leather boots reaching to just below the knee. They were laced

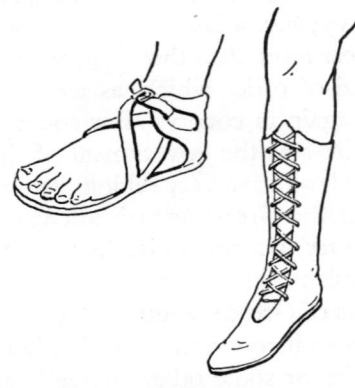

Greek sandal and boot

up the front, or else bound on the leg by means of leather thongs.

When men were doing hard agricultural work they seem sometimes to have worn gloves, probably of leather. Homer tells us that the father of Ulysses was working in the garden and wearing gloves when his son returned from his wanderings. Some Greeks and Romans, too, wore gloves at meal times, to keep their hands clean and so that they should not burn them with hot food, for they ate with their fingers.

Perhaps it is because we are familiar with Greek statues that we are inclined to think of Greek men and women as being clothed always in white or very pale tints. But actually their garments were of all kinds of bright colours, such as yellow, green, dark red, violet and dark purple (all of which are mentioned by Homer), as well as the duller browns and dark greens which are found in all countries where peasants weave their own fabrics and dye them with dyes made from plants and earths.

We know, too, that fabrics had coloured patterns woven into or embroidered on to them, as those found at Kertch and Athens had. But the Greeks did not smother themselves with gold and jewels as the Assyrians and some other ancient peoples did. After the earliest times men seem to have worn hardly any jewels except rings engraved with a seal, but women wore necklaces and bracelets, long pins, ear-rings and hair ornaments of gold. Both sexes wore 'fibulae', which were brooches something like safety-pins, to fasten their garments on the shoulders.

A Greek fibula or brooch

CHAPTER 6

Clothes in Northern Europe

While great civilizations were rising and falling in south-eastern Europe, northern Africa and Asia, what was happening in the colder, bleaker lands of northern Europe, and in Britain?

How were the people dressed who, perhaps about four thousand years ago, cultivated the first small fields ever known in Britain, and made the oldest of the long barrows we can still see on the downs? Or the people who, about 1800 B.C., brought bronze into the country, and erected Stonehenge, Avebury and many smaller stone circles? Or the various Celtic tribes who introduced iron into Britain, about 500 B.C., and were finally overcome by the Roman conquerors?

None of these people left statues, wall-paintings, seals or books behind them from which we can learn what they looked like. So far as the earliest people are concerned we can only guess that they wore garments made of skins, perhaps sewn together by means of bone needles, and that, after they had learnt how to spin and weave, they wrapped themselves in rectangular strips of fabric much as the earliest peoples of other countries did.

But, by a strange chance, we *do* know something definite about the way the people of northern Europe dressed in the Bronze Age. Surprising as it may seem, the oldest everyday clothes that have survived till the present day belonged not to people of one of the great pre-Christian civilizations, but to people who lived in the land we now call Denmark more than a thousand years before the birth of Christ.

Bronze Age chieftains and their wives were buried, fully

dressed, in coffins made from hollowed-out tree-trunks. Some of these have been dug up from the peat-bogs of Denmark, and the clothes have been found intact, preserved just as they were when their owners were dressed in them for the last time over three thousand years ago.

The clothes were all made of loosely woven wool. Men wore a mantle over the shoulders and a kind of tunic made by wrapping a rectangular piece of material round them, wide enough to cover their bodies from armpits to knees. Leather thongs stitched to the top of the material were probably passed over the shoulders. Round the waist a leather or woven belt was

A bronze-age man and girl

worn, and in front of the belt was a large, round, bronze plate, decorated with a spiral pattern. On their heads the men wore woollen caps, and on their feet sandals or shoes made from a piece of leather with a leather thong fastened at the back and threaded round the edge, thus drawing the shoe up like a bag or purse over the foot.

The women wore waist-length bodices of the usual T-shape, with skirts over them. The sleeves of the bodices came about to the elbows. The skirts, like the men's tunics, were simply pieces of material wrapped round the body, reaching to the ankles, and held in position by a belt similar to the men's, or by a long cord twisted twice round the waist and knotted in front. But sometimes the skirt consisted of a large number of cords or threads, tied in knots at intervals and hanging loosely from the bodice about to the wearer's knees. Women as well as men wore the large round bronze discs or buckles, and the leather sandals, and women confined their hair in a net, and held it in position with long bronze pins.

It seems very likely that the people living in Britain at this time wore clothes very like those worn by their neighbours just across the North Sea. No actual clothes have been found in Britain, but fragments of both linen and wool have survived in

A necklace of tin, faience and amber

A jet necklet and an armlet

Bronze Age barrows, showing that the people were familiar with flax and knew how to make it into linen. And many ornaments have been found, such as amber and jet beads and necklaces, bangles, brooches, gold buckles, and even faience beads (the blue beads that came from Egypt) which show us that trade was far more extensive three thousand years ago than we sometimes realize.

CLOTHES IN NORTHERN EUROPE

Of the men of the Iron Age—the Celts who began to invade Britain from the continent about 500 B.C.—we know a little more because, by this time, traders from the Mediterranean sometimes brought men with them who were capable of writing descriptions of the things and people they saw, and such descriptions have sometimes survived. For instance, about 325 B.C. a Greek explorer named Pytheas reached the coast of Cornwall, and wrote a description of the way in which the people mined and prepared tin, which they sold to the traders. And less than two hundred years later the Romans under Julius Caesar, after they had overcome the country we now call France and which they called Gaul, landed in Britain, though it was not until a century later that Britain fell entirely under the domination of Rome.

The Celts wove their materials in bright colours and in checked and striped patterns that may have been something like the tartans that are still woven in Scotland. The men sometimes wrapped a piece of knee-length material round their bodies as the Bronze Age men had done, and kept it in position by means of a belt. The lower part formed a kind of kilt, which has also survived in Scotland. Round their legs they might wrap pieces of cloth or soft leather, tying them on at ankle and knee. But the Celts also introduced into Britain for the first time the garments that we saw being worn in far-away Persia—long, loose trousers. They had holes round the waist through which a cord or leather thong was threaded to hold them in place, and they were also drawn in at the ankles with thongs. The trousers were made of wool or linen or sometimes of leather.

A Celtic man

Men also wore sleeveless tunics, or T-shaped tunics with short or, occasionally, with long sleeves, and cloaks of cloth or fur which were fastened

63

on the right shoulder with brooches of bronze, gold or enamel. They wore their hair long and grew big moustaches, though they did not often wear beards.

They were very fond of wearing an ornament called a 'torque'. It was worn round the neck and was made of twisted gold wire. Bracelets of the same kind were very popular too.

A chieftain, when he was dressed for fighting, would wear a bronze breastplate over his tunic, and a bronze helmet on his head. His belt would support his iron sword, and he would

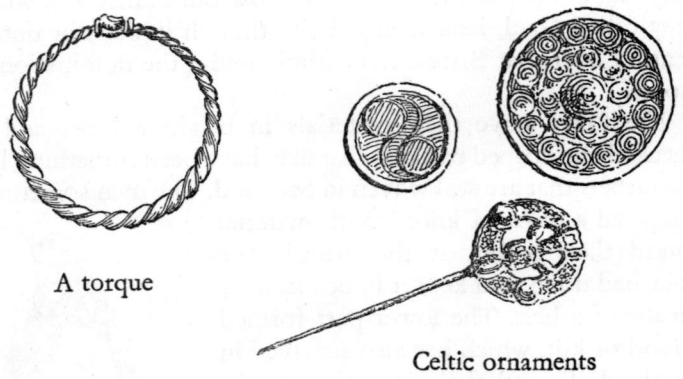

A torque

Celtic ornaments

carry an oval shield which, like the belt, might be richly decorated with red enamel. He might wear the trousers (or bracco, as they were called) but in war-time he would be more likely to be bare-legged.

Women wore the ankle-length, T-shaped tunics that we have met in so many places, and both sexes wore bangles, necklaces, rings and beads. Brooches were very common. Some were circular and some were of the safety-pin type.

On their feet men and women wore soft leather bag-shaped shoes, similar to those worn in the Bronze Age.

People dressed in clothes such as these met and resisted the Romans when they landed in Britain in A.D. 43. A few years later, in A.D. 51, such clothes were seen in Rome itself when the captured and defeated Briton, Caractacus, many of his followers, and all his family, were led in triumph through the streets.

Even then resistance was not at an end in Britain, and ten years later Boudicca, the chieftainess of the Iceni (whom we usually call Boadicea), led a Celtic rising against the conquerors. It was successful for a time, and thousands of Roman men, women and children were killed. But in the end Boudicca and her followers were defeated and Boudicca poisoned herself rather than be taken a prisoner to Rome.

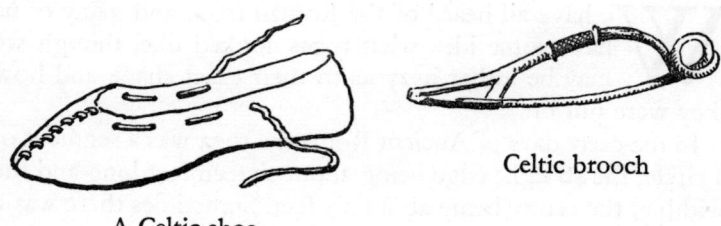

Celtic brooch

A Celtic shoe

A Greek historian named Dion Cassius has left us a description of Boudicca as she appeared when leading her followers into battle. He says she was very tall and grim looking, with keen eyes and a harsh voice, and that she had a great deal of very yellow hair hanging down her back and reaching far below her waist. She wore a great golden collar, and bracelets on her arms and wrists. Her long tunic hung in folds round her and was of several colours, chiefly blue, red and yellow. She wore a sagum (cloak) over it, fastened by a fibula (brooch). She carried a spear in her hand.

Long after the Romans had built their cities and villas, their camps, roads and theatres in Britain, men and women wearing the native dress must have been seen in their hundreds, mingling with the Romans in their togas.

CHAPTER 7

The Reign of the Toga

We have all heard of the Roman toga, and many of us have some idea what togas looked like, though we may be rather hazy as to their exact shape and how they were put on.

In the early days of Ancient Rome the toga was a segment of a circle, the straight edge being about sixteen feet long and the width at the centre being about six feet. Sometimes there was a

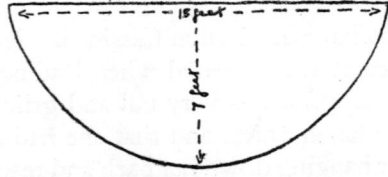

Diagram of a toga

coloured border round the curved edge, but later on it was the straight edge that had a border, if any, and the toga was bigger —about eighteen and a half feet along the straight edge and seven feet deep in the centre.

The toga was put on in this way. The straight edge was placed against the neck with one point hanging down to the ground in front, from the left shoulder. The rest of the garment was taken across the back, under the right arm, across the chest and over the left shoulder so that the other point hung down the back. Then part of the toga which hung down in front was drawn up in a loop over the part that crossed the body in front.

The best way to understand this is to dress yourself, or some-

66

one else, in a toga if you can get hold of a piece of material large enough; if not, try putting it on a doll or puppet.

At first all Roman men and women appear to have worn the toga, but later it became the recognized dress of freemen and aristocrats. Women gave it up. Peasants, slaves, servants and others of the lower orders were not allowed to wear it; neither

How the toga was put on

were Romans who had been outlawed or disgraced. Foreigners could only wear the toga after they had been accepted as Roman citizens.

There were several different kinds of togas. The one worn by the ordinary citizen was nearly always of natural (creamy) coloured wool, and was usually undecorated. People in mourning wore black or very dark togas, and those who were candidates for public office wore plain white ones.

People in important positions, such as magistrates, consuls and senators, wore a large toga which was folded over along the straight edge before it was put on, and which had a purple border along the edge of the folded-over part. This part of the toga was drawn up over the head when the wearer was taking part in a religious ceremony. We can picture Pontius Pilate wearing a toga of this kind when he was trying Christ.

The colour purple (which was probably much redder than the colour we call purple now, and more like crimson) was a sign of rank, because purple dye was rare and expensive. It was made by the Phoenicians, whose chief town was Tyre on the Mediterranean, from a little sea-creature called the murex. So the colour was usually called Tyrian purple.

Curiously enough, the toga praetexta, as the purple-bordered toga was called, was also worn by boys until they were about sixteen years old, when they had to give it up and wear the ordinary toga of the citizen. At the coming-of-age ceremonies boys wore a special white tunic, and they took off from round their necks a kind of locket, called a bulla, which they had worn from earliest babyhood. It contained a lucky charm, or amulet. The bulla was of gold if the boy was the son of rich parents; otherwise it was of leather.

Generals, when they made a triumphal entry into Rome after a victorious campaign, were clothed in an elaborate toga that belonged to the State, made of purple cloth embroidered in gold. It was called a toga picta. Later, emperors wore this toga picta as an official dress.

Augurs, the men who were supposed to be able to foretell the future and to advise people when the time was right for any particular action, wore togas with scarlet stripes and a purple edge.

In the earliest days of Ancient Rome men wore nothing else but the toga, but after about 300 B.C. they began to wear a tunic under it. Men's tunics were often short, and either of the familiar T-shape with short sleeves, or rectangular, with spaces left in the sides for the arms to go through (not in the top edge, as with the Greeks). The Romans at this time hated the idea of having their arms covered, so, although they copied the Greeks in most things, they did not, for a long time, adopt the long sleeves which Alexander the Great introduced into Greece after his Persian campaign. The earlier Romans regarded such things as sleeves to cover the arms and trousers to cover the legs as unmanly, and at the same time as characteristic of barbarians. But later the long sleeve did become more popular and by Nero's time (A.D. 37–68) it was quite common.

Older men, and men in official positions, and women, wore an ankle-length tunic called the 'tunica talaris'. Sometimes men wore an under-tunic under the upper one, and we are told that the Emperor Octavius, who was evidently a very chilly person, wore as many as four tunics, and he even wrapped pieces of cloth round his legs to keep them warm.

Tunics were generally of plain wool or linen, cream or white, but sometimes they had one purple stripe (called a clavus) down the centre of the back and front. The clavus was two fingers in width, and is said to have been adopted by Roman senators about the seventh century B.C. as a badge of office. Later two clavi, one on either side of both back and front of the tunic, were worn by knights. About the end of the first century A.D. the clavi ceased to be regarded as badges of rank, and were used simply as ornament. They played an important part in the clothes of early Christian times and later.

Roman wearing a tunic decorated with the clavus, and a cloak

Tunics worn with the purple toga picta by victorious generals were very elaborately embroidered all over in gold, and were themselves purple. This kind of tunic was called a 'tunica palmata'. On his head the victorious general wore a laurel wreath, and in his right hand he carried a laurel branch. In his left hand he carried an ivory sceptre with an eagle on it. Twelve men, called lictors, attended him, all wearing red tunics, and with laurel wreaths on their heads.

The emperors, from Nero onwards, wore the tunica palmata as their usual dress.

The tunics of working men were knee-length and sleeveless, and the right arm was often drawn out of its arm-hole, leaving the shoulder and arm bare, when there was hard work to be done.

Soldiers wore cuirasses, which were sometimes of metal, but were probably more often of leather covered with overlapping scales or links of metal. Under them they wore short red tunics, and those who served in the chilly countries of northern Europe took to wearing bracco, or breeches—though the Romans despised such barbarian garments and the soldiers were careful not to wear them when they re-entered Rome.

Men such as soldiers and horsemen sometimes wore a rectangular woollen cloak like the Greek chlamys, about four feet wide by eight feet long, folded double and fastened with a brooch on the right shoulder. In colder countries such as France and Britain the Romans sometimes wore a similar cloak but of thicker coarser wool, with a hood.

Another kind of cloak worn by countrymen or travellers was circular, or nearly circular, with a hole for the head to go through—though occasionally it was open up the front and fastened with clasps. It could be any length from hips to ankles and often had a hood attached. It was called a paenula. Almost exactly the same kind of cloak, made of thick, hairy wool, is still worn by men in the mountains of Austria and other parts of central Europe. The paenula is important because of the part it played in the clothes of later times.

Roman men generally went bare-headed (though soldiers, of course, wore helmets) and they are usually shown with their short hair combed down all round their heads, with a fringe across the forehead.

As we have seen, women did not wear togas. Their clothes were almost exactly like those of the Greek women, though the garments had different names. The Ionic chiton of the Greeks became the Roman stola, and the Greek himation became, in Rome, the palla. The stola might be a T-shaped garment with elbow sleeves, but the shoulder seams would not be sewn up, but attached to one another with brooches. It might, however, have straight sides with openings for the arms, and therefore be sleeveless, in which case the under-tunic which women wore might have long sleeves—but not both garments.

The palla, or big rectangular cloak of wool, could be draped in many ways. It usually started as the toga did by being placed over the left shoulder and hanging down to the ground in front. Then the rest of it was drawn across the back and either over or under the right arm, finishing by hanging over the left arm. Sometimes the upper edge was folded over before the draping started, so that the folded-back part could be drawn up over the head when necessary. Sometimes the palla was wrapped twice round the body, fairly tightly, and the arms and even the hands might be completely swathed in it.

The clothes worn by Roman men and women did not change much for centuries, but at last, towards the end of the first century A.D., the toga, after seven hundred years, began to lose its popularity. Roman citizens began to wear cloaks that were easier to put on and to manage. But the toga was still used for ceremonial purposes, and as the official wear of magistrates, senators and other high officials. The richly decorated toga picta worn over the tunica palmata was recognized as the official garb of the emperor, and later, of Roman consuls. Towards the end of the fourth century A.D., by which time the toga had been

almost completely discarded by ordinary men, laws were passed ordering magistrates and senators to wear it when they were performing their duties. That kind of thing is not at all uncommon—that the clothes of a previous age survive for ceremonial, legal, religious and regal purposes. Our own judges and lawyers still wear wigs and gowns, generations after they have been discarded by other men.

The toga in its last form was richly decorated and folded into a strip which was wrapped round the figure and only loosened for the last yard or two, where it came across the front of the wearer and over the left elbow.

Toga as worn in later times

The Roman tunic did not alter until

towards the end of the second century, when it became usual to gather the neck fulness into a narrow neckband. About this time, too, certain frivolous young men began, occasionally, to wear the type of tunic that was worn farther east, fuller and wider than the Roman one, unbelted and with long, wide sleeves.

These foreign fashions were strongly disapproved of, and when the Emperor Commodus appeared in such clothes in A.D. 190 most Romans were shocked and disgusted. However, twenty-six years later they had more cause for anger, for the Emperor Heliogabalus made his State entry into Rome dressed in one of these full, wide-sleeved garments. It was of purple silk, embroidered in gold, and round his neck the emperor wore a jewelled collar and ropes of pearls. We are told that his face was made up in pink and white, and that his eyes and eyebrows were tinged with black.

It was not only the fact that the clothes the emperor wore were in a foreign style that annoyed the Romans, but the fact that he was clothed entirely in pure Chinese silk, which they thought was grossly extravagant. Silk, from thick satin to the finest transparent veiling, was popular among wealthy Romans, but it was still scarce and enormously expensive, since the Chinese were still the only people who knew how to produce it.

But about this time their three-thousand-year-old secret began to leak out. The Japanese were the first to learn it. They sent men to China who persuaded, bribed or forced four Chinese silk weavers to go to Japan, where they taught the Japanese all they knew. Not much later, about A.D. 300, a Chinese princess is said to have taken the secret to India. She went as bride to an Indian prince and in one of her head-dresses she concealed some silkworm eggs.

Not long after Heliogabalus startled the Romans with his foreign fashions, the dalmatica, as the new-shaped tunic was called (because the Romans had adopted it from Dalmatia) became the usual wear for most Romans. It was really only the T-shaped tunic which we have met before, but made rather wide and with long sleeves at least ten inches, and often more, across.

It was worn without any belt or girdle, and sometimes reached to just below the knee, when worn by men. It might be worn alone, or it might have a tunic under it. From the middle of the third century onwards the tunic was given long, close-fitting sleeves, and was embroidered in wool where it showed beneath the dalmatica, that is at neck, wrists and hem. Sometimes the long-sleeved tunic was worn by itself.

The clavi (the coloured stripes back and front from shoulder to hem) decorated the dalmatica, or the tunic if it was worn alone. And tunics, if they were worn without the dalmatica, were often decorated with 'segmentae'—circles or squares of embroidery on each shoulder, and one on each side of the front and back of the garment, near the hem. The clavi and the segmentae remained popular forms of decoration for hundreds of years. In fact, they have survived to the present day in certain Greek islands.

Women, like men, took to wearing the dalmatica. At first they wore the sleeveless stola under it, but later they added long, close-fitting sleeves to the stola and called it a camisia. There was little difference between the clothes worn by men and women.

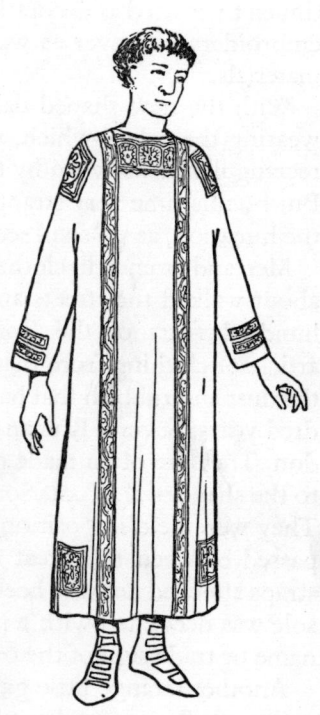

Tunic with clavi and segmentae

When they were wearing the full, loose, long-sleeved dalmatica, women found it was not easy to drape the palla, or cloak, over it, so for a time they discarded the palla altogether and took to wearing a light wool or silk or cotton veil over their heads and shoulders instead.

Early in the fourth century the dalmatica changed its shape a little. Instead of being made with straight sides, so that it was the same width all the way up, and with sleeves the same width from shoulder to wrist, it was now cut with seams that sloped outwards from under the arms. This meant that the garment fitted more closely to the wearer's waist, though it was still full round the hem, and the sleeves widened out towards the wrist. The clavi, in plain colours, or embroidered in patterns, continued to be used as decoration, but the dalmatica was now often embroidered all over as well, or was woven in rich patterned materials.

With the new shaped dalmatica women took once more to wearing the palla—which, you remember, was the same as the rectangular cloak worn by the Greeks and called the himation. But by this time very strange things indeed were happening to the himation, as we shall see.

Men and women in clothes such as you have just been reading about walked the streets and tracks of Britain during the four hundred years of the Roman occupation. Sometimes some article of clothing from that distant time is found buried under the dust and rubbish that has been accumulating for fifteen hundred years. Several Roman sandals have been found near London. They are often made of several thicknesses of leather, cut to the shape of the foot. Sometimes they are studded with nails. They were held in position by straps, one of which sometimes passed between the great and second toes to join two other straps attached near the heel. Sometimes the upper surface of the sole was decorated with a pattern made with a hot iron, or the name or trade sign of the owner was put there.

Another strange little garment was found recently in the remains of a Roman well excavated in London, in which there was also pottery, glass, bronze articles, and a Roman ladder. The garment was a pair of drawers made of soft goat's skin. It was laced up at the sides, and was very small, not more than about two inches deep at each side and across the centre. There are in existence in Sicily some Roman mosaic pictures showing girl athletes wearing garments similar to this one, but experts believe that the one found in London was probably worn by a slave girl, and that it was all the clothing she had. If so, she must often have wished that her owner lived in the sunny south of Italy instead of in chilly, wet England.

This little garment, as well as Roman sandals and many other interesting things, can be seen at the Guildhall Museum in London.

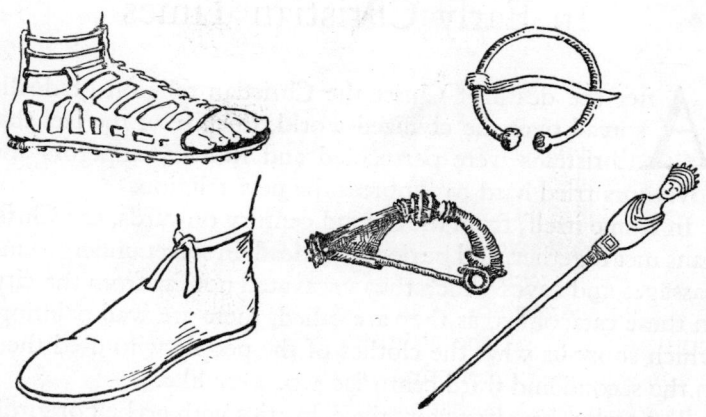

Roman sandal and shoe   Roman brooches and pin

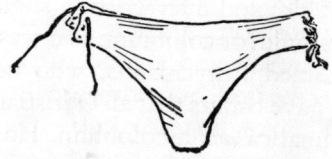

Leather garment of Roman times
found in London

CHAPTER 8

In Early Christian Times

After the death of Christ the Christian religion gradually spread over the civilized world, in spite of the fact that Christians were persecuted and Roman emperors and governors tried hard to suppress the new religion.

In Rome itself, from the second century onwards, the Christians met together, and buried their dead, in secret underground passages and caves which they excavated not far from the city. In these catacombs, as they are called, there are wall paintings which show us what the clothes of the people who used them in the second and third centuries A.D. were like.

The early Christians wore the dalmatica with no belt or girdle and with the clavi in deep red or purple. Both men and women are shown on the walls of the catacombs, women wearing the dalmatica to the ankles and men wearing slightly shorter ones. As a rule no under-tunic (or colobium, as it was called) is shown, but a Christian named Entychianus, who became Bishop of Rome in A.D. 275, gave orders that all Christian martyrs were to be buried in a dalmatica *and* a colobium. He himself died the death of a martyr in A.D. 283.

Another garment that frequently appears in the catacombs is the paenula, the circular, or nearly circular, cloak which had been worn for centuries by peasants and other humble people, and by travellers. In the catacombs the paenula, like the dalmatica, is usually decorated with the two clavi.

Among the persecuted Christians of Roman times were two brothers named Crispin and Crispianus. There are several versions of their story. In one they are said to have been born in Rome in the reign of Diocletian, and to have fled to avoid persecution, later becoming shoemakers in Soissons. Later they were captured and several ways of killing them were tried, including placing them in a cauldron of boiling oil. But nothing harmed them until they were finally beheaded and buried in Soissons.

According to another much more cheerful version, they were born in Canterbury, the sons of the Queen of Kent. Having be-

A man in a tunic, dalmatica and cloak from the Catacombs

Man in a paenula, from the Catacombs

come Christian they fled in disguise to Faversham, where they became shoemakers. Later Crispin, while fitting the emperor's daughter, Ursula, with shoes, fell in love with her and she with him. They were married secretly by a blind priest under an oak tree, and later Crispin and his brother Crispianus (who had done great things while fighting with the Roman army) were accepted and honoured by the emperor. In this version of the story they died peacefully and were buried at Faversham.

Whichever version, if either, is true, the two brothers became the patron saints of shoemakers, and pictures of them, or of scenes from one or other of their stories, appear on the arms of shoemakers' guilds in many places in different parts of Europe.

Early in the fourth century Constantine the Great was converted to Christianity, and in A.D. 323 Christianity became the state religion of the Roman Empire. Churches began to spring up everywhere, many of them decorated with pictures, mosaics and sculptures in which men and women dressed in the clothes of the time appear.

At this time Greece, although it had lost its independence in 146 B.C. and become subject to Rome, remained the leader of the civilized world in culture and learning. The Greeks, you remember, wore over their chitons (or tunics) the large rectangular himation—not the toga of the Romans. People who were influenced by Greek culture and thought also wore the himation, and even in Rome it was worn by philosophers, teachers, orators and learned men generally. It was regarded as a badge of learning—a garment of dignity and honour.

For this reason Christian artists, when they began to depict Christ, the Disciples, St. Paul and the many saints and martyrs, showed them wearing himations draped over tunics—not togas, which had been worn by the Romans who had persecuted the Christians, and not the Hebrew clothes which some of the Bible characters must have worn when they were alive.

Quite early in the fourth century Pope Silvester decreed that deacons (that is to say, servants of the Church) should wear a dalmatica over a long tunic (colobium) when taking part in the church services, and by the middle of the fourth century it was usual for bishops to wear the tunic, the dalmatica, and the paenula. But there was nothing unusual or special about these clothes—they were the ordinary everyday clothes of the common people at that time, though they continued to be venerated, after fashions changed, because they had been worn by the early Christian martyrs. It was when these particular garments had been discarded for ordinary wear that, as they continued to be worn by the clergy, they became recognized as Church vestments.

A popular name for the paenula was 'casula', which means a little house or hut, because it covered the wearer entirely, except for his head, like a tent. In time the word 'casula' changed to 'chasuble', and that is the name by which a cloak-like garment with no front opening which is worn by certain clergymen is called. But the chasuble has changed its shape a great deal during the hundreds of years that have passed since the early Christians wore it in the form of the paenula.

About the middle of the fourth century the rectangular Greek himation, or pallium as the Romans called it, began to lose favour, just as the toga had done a century or so earlier. It remained in use as an official garment for people occupying certain positions, but was worn differently. Men took to folding it lengthwise into a long strip about twelve or fifteen inches wide, which they then wrapped round them as they had done the original garment—over the left shoulder, across the back, under the right arm and up over the left shoulder again. As a badge of office it was worn over the paenula by officers of the Senate, according to a decree of A.D. 382.

When the narrow, folded pallium was worn over the paenula it was, of course, not possible to bring it forward *under* the right arm, and it had therefore to be brought over the shoulder and so formed a kind of loose collar.

Before long the unnecessary material of the pallium was discarded altogether, and it became simply a long strip of material, often of two colours, twelve to fifteen inches wide and fifteen to eighteen feet long.

As time passed the pallium became narrower still—about four inches wide, and it came to be especially associated with the Church, and particularly with the Pope. It was worn over the chasuble, and was held in position by three pins, one at the back, one in front, and one on the left shoulder, where the two portions crossed.

From about the seventh century onwards the strip of cloth or silk of which the pallium was made was shaped into a circle with a piece hanging down the back and front. From the eighth century the pallium became a special vestment which was conferred by the Pope on archbishops, and occasionally on bishops, as a great honour. If they proved unworthy they were obliged to return it. Each pallium, before it was sent to the man who was to receive it, was placed on the shoulders of the Pope himself.

Later still the circle became two V-shaped pieces, and the

A folded pallium
over a paenula

The ecclesiastical
pallium

pallium, now only about three inches wide, was decorated with six crosses, three in front and three at the back. In this form it is still worn by archbishops of the Roman Catholic Church. In the Greek Church a similar pallium is worn, but much wider.

The pallium, the chasuble, and other similar garments, such as copes (which are semi-circular cloaks, open up the front), surplices, cassocks, all of which are worn by clergymen when they are taking part in certain church services, are examples of the way in which ordinary every-day clothes gradually became the special garments used for ceremonies.

Gloves, too, became part of the dress of the clergy in early Christian times. The priest wore gloves at Mass, and it became the custom, at least from the sixth century, for a bishop at his consecration to be given a pair of gloves, as a sign that he must perform his duties with clean hands. In time gloves were worn only by bishops, and lesser clergy were not allowed to wear them. Bishops' gloves were usually of silk and were embroidered on the backs with a gold cross, or some other symbol of Christianity.

CHAPTER 9

At the Byzantine Court

In A.D. 330 Constantine the Great founded Constantinople on the site of the ancient city of Byzantium, and in A.D. 395, when the Roman Empire was divided into two parts, an eastern and a western, Constantinople became the capital of the eastern empire. After the collapse of the Roman Empire in the west in A.D. 476 Constantinople became the chief city of the civilized world for culture and learning. This eastern part of the Roman Empire is called the Byzantine Empire.

By this time, the fifth century A.D., the richly decorated toga picta worn over the long, richly embroidered tunica palmata had ceased to be the official garb of the emperors. Mosaics in ancient churches, and the miniatures in religious books that have survived from these early times, show the emperors wearing knee-length tunics with long close sleeves, and with a belt or girdle rather low round the waist or hips. The tunic is usually slit up a little at each side, and is decorated on each shoulder with embroidered or woven segmentae, in squares or circles, and also round the wrists and across the bottom edge, back and front.

As a rule the emperors went bare-legged, but some men at this time were beginning to wear bracco, or trousers, in spite of attempts by the authorities to stop them. Emperors both of the eastern and western empires made laws prohibiting the wearing of such 'barbarian' garments under threat of banishment and loss of goods.

Over the tunic the emperors are shown wearing a long cloak to the ankles, fastened on the right shoulder with an elaborate jewelled brooch. This cloak was probably semi-circular, like the copes worn by certain clergymen to-day, but it probably had a curved piece cut out in the centre of the long straight edge, so that it fitted fairly closely at the neck. The cloak was called a paludamentum.

The paludamentum Byzantine emperors wore on state occasions was purple, and at first it was always of plain material, though of the richest, heaviest silk obtainable. But it was always ornamented in a certain way. Two squares or oblongs of brilliant embroidered and jewelled decoration were placed on the edge of the cloak, one at the back and one at the front. This decoration was called the 'tablion'.

The paludamentum, decorated with the tablion, was worn by men of the court, and by high officials, but only the emperor's paludamentum was purple with a gold tablion. High officials wore white paludamentums with purple tablions, and the colours worn by lesser officials depended on their rank. After the eighth century empresses also wore the purple paludamentum and tablions, but not other women. Women still wore the himation, or else a semi-circular cloak over their tunics.

Until the sixth century the rich silk fabrics which wealthy and important men and women loved to wear had to be imported at great expense from Persia and countries farther east, or woven from raw silk brought all the way from China. But one day two Persian monks who had been to China as missionaries came to the Emperor Justinian in Constantinople and told him that they had mastered the whole art of silk production. He promised them great rewards if they could bring silkworms to Constantinople and enable the people of the Byzantine empire to manufacture silk for themselves.

The two men returned to China and in spite of the watchfulness of the Chinese they managed to smuggle some silkworms' eggs out of the country, hidden in a bamboo tube. They reached Constantinople with their precious loot in A.D. 551. For six hundred years after that the people of the Byzantine Empire managed to keep the silkworms to themselves. Byzantine silk factories produced wonderful silken fabrics, some interwoven with gold and silver thread, and nearly all woven in elaborate patterns in which animals, birds, human beings, dragons, hunting scenes, and so on, appeared.

At first silken fabrics were manufactured in the imperial palace itself, under the control of the emperor. The finest materials were kept for the use of the emperor and his court, and no one was allowed to sell them to foreign countries. The emperors would make presents of fine silks to those foreign kings and nobles they especially wanted to please. The silks that were exported were very expensive indeed and could only be bought by the wealthiest.

The sixth century is celebrated for something else besides the fact that the silkworm reached the western world for the first time. Also for the first time the men of a highly civilized western empire adopted the garments they had despised for so long and which we know as breeches or trousers. For centuries trousers had been regarded as the distinctive wear of barbarians, such as the Gauls and Celts of northern Europe, or foreigners such as the Persians. Now men of the upper classes in the Byzantine Empire, from the emperor downwards, took to wearing close-fitting leg coverings, something like modern tights, which they called hosa.

In a church in Ravenna there are some wonderful mosaics in which the Emperor Justinian and his wife Theodora are shown with members of their court. The emperor is wearing a white knee-length tunic, girdled round the waist and decorated with the segmentae embroidered in gold. His purple paludamentum is lined with

The Emperor Justinian

reddish coloured silk, and is fastened on the right shoulder with a jewel from which three strings of pearls hang. The tablion has a gold ground and a pattern of small birds in circles. On his legs the emperor is wearing close-fitting purple silk trousers, or hosa, and on his feet red shoes trimmed with pearls. The men with Justinian are dressed in very much the

The Empress Theodora and a lady-in-waiting

same way, but their clothes are less elaborately decorated. An archbishop is shown wearing an ankle-length tunic with the wide-sleeved dalmatica over it, which is decorated with the clavi and with two narrow stripes on the sleeve. Over it he wears the chasuble, and round his shoulders, over the chasuble, comes the ecclesiastical pallium.

The Empress Theodora is shown wearing a gold embroidered

tunic similar to the emperor's but reaching her ankles, and over it a purple cloak lined with blue. Round the bottom of the cloak is a wide strip of gold embroidery representing the Adoration of the Magi, or Wise Men. Round her neck the empress wears a deep jewelled collar, a little like those worn by the Egyptians hundreds of years earlier. The ladies with her are dressed in long tunics, with cloaks which were probably rectangular himations, draped over them and drawn closely round their necks and shoulders. Both garments, in some cases, are made of materials with woven patterns all over them. The tunic of one lady is decorated with the clavi in gold, for this form of decoration was still popular. But by this time, for men, the stripes were often cut short and ended just above the waist. These short clavi were not worn by women.

As time went on the clothes worn at the Byzantine court became more and more extravagant and magnificent. Cloth-of-gold and precious stones of all kinds were used lavishly, so that the clothes were often stiff and heavy with them. An emperor in his state robes had to hold himself as rigidly as a statue.

After a time the wide-sleeved dalmatica, showing the fitted sleeve of the under tunic, came back into favour for both sexes, and both garments were often ankle length. The paludamentum, which was still worn, was now often made of brocade, or was embroidered all over, and the tablion was a mass of gold and jewels.

From the eighth to the twelfth centuries the long strip of material which had developed from the toga and the himation, and which had become the pallium worn by Popes and archbishops, was also very often worn at the Byzantine court. This civilian pallium (which was sometimes called the lorum) was from nine to twelve inches wide and was gorgeously decorated with gold, jewels, and, quite often, a fringe of pearls on both sides along the whole of its eighteen feet or so of length. It was arranged in various ways, and sometimes simply had a hole for the head to go through and hung straight down behind and in front of the wearer.

The richness and the splendour of the clothes worn by Byzantine nobles have never been surpassed. The shapes of the actual garments remained simple, and those worn by ordinary everyday people were probably quite plain, or simply decorated with coloured embroidery or woven patterns. But for the nobility nothing was too lavish. The grave of one of the Byzantine empresses was opened in 1544, and it was found that she was wrapped in a shroud of cloth-of-gold which, when it was melted down, was found to contain thirty-six pounds of pure gold.

From about the tenth century men of the Byzantine court took to wearing hats with high, round crowns and upstanding brims, or sometimes with soft, pointed crowns which hung over the side of the head and had a tassel on the end. Some-

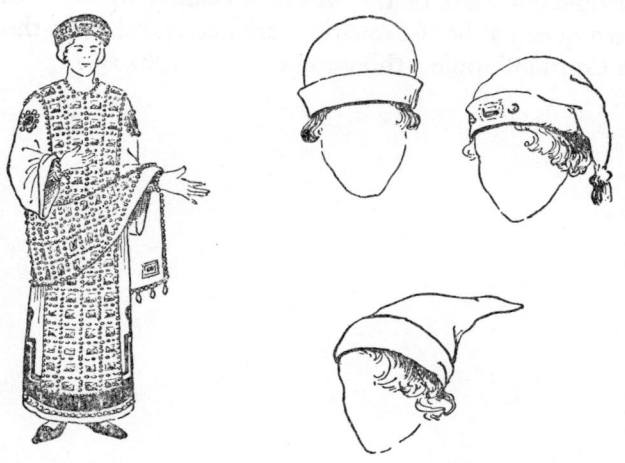

Another version of the pallium   Byzantine heads

times the brim was of fur, or of silk or some rich material, embroidered and set with jewels. Hats of this kind, and of course much simpler ones for poorer people, remained in use for some hundreds of years in countries that had been part of, or influenced by, the Byzantine empire.

From about the tenth century, too, men took to wearing a kind of sock, or loose boot, over their close-fitting hosa. These 'pedules', as they were called, were of soft leather or cloth. Sometimes, when they were of cloth, shoes were worn over them with long thongs attached which were criss-crossed up the leg, over the pedules. Some men wore long loose breeches instead of the close-fitting hosa, and cross-gartered them up to the knee.

These pedules, and the cross-gartering, were adopted from the tribes which had overrun northern Europe, the Franks and Teutons, amongst whom the short tunic, long trousers, pedules and knee-length cloak, often fastened on the right shoulder, were generally worn.

The Byzantine court influenced every other court in Europe, as we shall see, and many of the ceremonial garments still worn in different parts of the world, including those worn by our own queen at her Coronation, are descended from those worn in Constantinople a thousand or more years ago.

CHAPTER 10

The Clothes of the 'Barbarians'

We have seen how contact with the tribes which had overrun the western half of the Roman Empire caused the citizens of the eastern, or Byzantine, part, in time, to adopt certain of their garments—such as the bracco, or trousers.

The opposite also happened—the conquerors changed their mode of dress to some extent in imitation of the Romans. We are told by Tacitus, who lived in the first century A.D., that the Teuton tribes of his time often wore clothes of fur or leather, and that when they wore linen or woollen tunics they were narrow, close-fitting and sleeveless, fastened on the shoulder, and short for men, ankle-length for women.

After the collapse of the Roman Empire in the west in the fifth century A.D. we hear of certain Teutons in Italy wearing wider and longer tunics in the Roman style, gaily decorated with embroidery, and over them green cloaks with wide purple hems.

When, early in the sixth century, the Frankish king, Clovis, made himself master of the country which had been called Gaul and which was later to be known as France, the Byzantine Emperor Anastatius conferred on him the title of Augustus. Gregory, who was Bishop of Tours from A.D. 573 until 594, and who wrote a history of Gaul, tells us that Clovis promptly dressed himself in the decorated tunic (knee length at that time) and paludamentum, or big cloak, worn by the Byzantine emperors. The chief men of his court followed his example. For generations after that Byzantine dress, custom and ceremonial were usual at the Frankish Court. But Clovis and his followers

89

continued to wear their hair long and flowing and they wore the long trousers which the Romans and Byzantines had not then adopted. They regarded long hair as a sign of freedom, and short hair as a badge of slavery.

Farther north, in Britain, the Angles, Saxons and Jutes had begun to invade the country after the departure of the Romans in A.D. 410. We are told that the invaders wore leather tunics over their woollen ones. The chiefs had metal rings or scales, perhaps gilded, sewn close together all over the leather, and wore helmets of iron or gilded bronze or made up of a metal

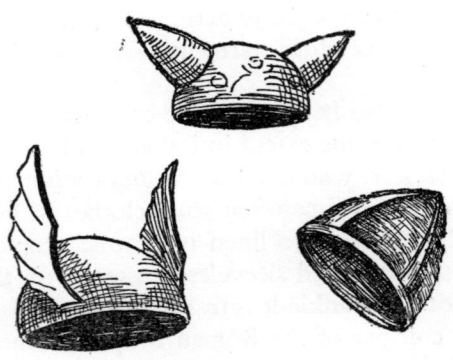

Saxon and Viking helmets

frame filled in with horn or leather, on their heads. Sometimes the most important chiefs had the outspread wings of an eagle attached one on each side of the helmet; sometimes a model in metal of a boar or other animal might be placed on the top; sometimes the helmet had horns sticking out on either side.

Hanging from their shoulders the invaders might wear a cloak of fur or cloth, and the humbler men might wear nothing but trousers and a cloak. On their feet the early Saxons wore simple bag-shaped shoes of leather, with long thongs attached, which were cross-gartered up to the knee over the trousers, or the cloth wrappings called socca, which they sometimes put round the lower leg.

THE CLOTHES OF THE 'BARBARIANS'

A chronicler tells us that Hengist, when he landed at Ebbs-fleet in A.D. 449, was wearing one of the leather tunics covered with metal scales, and a fur cloak, and that he carried a spear and a shield. Another chief wore the same kind of clothes, but had amber beads and a golden torque round his neck.

Both men and women had long hair flowing down on to their shoulders, or hanging in long plaits.

When St. Augustine arrived in Britain in A.D. 597 and began the conversion of the Saxons to Christianity he introduced, for clergymen, the robes which were worn by the clergy in Rome and Byzantium—the long white under-tunic which was called the alb, the slightly shorter wide-sleeved upper tunic, or dalmatica, the chasuble, and, in the case of archbishops, the pallium.

Later, when Christianity was established and churches had been built all over the country, we read of the richness of these ecclesiastical garments, and of the beautiful material of which they were woven and the wonderful embroidery with which they were decorated. We read of silken vestments interwoven with gold and precious stones, and of cloth-of-gold chasubles which shone like pure gold in the light of the church candles. A stole into which figures of saints and prophets were woven was found in the coffin of St. Cuthbert, who died in A.D. 687 but was not finally buried in his shrine at Durham until 995. His body was wrapped in five robes of embroidered silk.

A great many men and women retired to the convents that were founded all over England, and they, of course, wore simple gowns of wool or linen or goat's hair prescribed for them by the founders of their orders. At least, they should have done, but Alcuin, who was a very learned monk from York who lived at the court of Charlemagne at Aix-la-Chapelle for some time, in his letters to monks was constantly urging them to avoid luxury in dress. This seems to suggest that some of them were tempted by the bright colours and gay embroideries of the clothes they saw around them.

Not that the shapes of the garments worn by ordinary men and women altered much. Men went on wearing the knee-length tunic, sometimes split up at the sides, and with a band of embroidery round the wrist, neck and hem, and a belt round the waist. The sleeves were close-fitting, but were usually long enough to be pulled down over the hands in cold weather. They could be pushed up, and rucked from elbow to wrist, when necessary. Over the tunic was the short cloak, fastened as

Saxon man and woman

before on the right shoulder, and on the legs were either long trousers cross-gartered to the knee, or short breeches, with wrappings, or 'socca', to the knee. The leather thongs used as garters were often coloured or gilded and were sometimes studded with metal.

The men who prepared leather, the tanners, lived in the

THE CLOTHES OF THE 'BARBARIANS'

depths of the great forests which spread over a great part of Britain, for in countries where oak trees grew, oak bark was used more than anything else for tanning leather. Wild animals

Saxon shoe

such as wolves and boars also lived in the forests and there are many ancient stories about the terrifying adventures the tanners and their families had, and the wild, isolated lives they lived.

Cannock Chase, a great forest in the Midlands, was a place where many tanners congregated.

Saxon women dressed very much as the women of Rome had done in later times, in an ankle-length under-tunic with long sleeves which they called a smock, and an upper, slightly shorter one, with wider, shorter sleeves, like the dalmatica, which they called a gunna. Over them, when they went out, they wore a big cloak which was sometimes like the paenula of the Romans—a circle with a hole for the head to go through—and sometimes semi-circular. They always wore a covering over their heads—either a rectangular piece of material which was draped over the head and under the chin and had one or both ends thrown back over the shoulder, or a circle of linen, or, for wealthy people, silk, with a hole for the face. A head-band might be placed on the head over the veil.

The Saxons, both men and women, loved jewellery, and many brooches, necklaces, rings and other things have been found in Saxon graves. Some of the necklaces are of coloured stones such as yellow amber or purple amethyst, and some are of gold wire twisted into bead-like shapes. The Saxons were particularly fond of the red stones called garnets, and some magnificent brooches, buckles and clasps have been found, made of gold set with garnets and, sometimes, with the blue stone called lapis lazuli.

One of the greatest finds ever made in Britain was at Sutton Hoo in Suffolk, when a mound was excavated and it was discovered that inside it was a Saxon ship of the seventh century containing many wonderful treasures which we can now see in the British Museum.

93

THE CLOTHES OF THE 'BARBARIANS'

It is believed that the ship and the treasure belonged to a Saxon king and that they were buried as a memorial to him—though he himself was not buried with them. There were several silver bowls which had come from Byzantium, a huge silver dish, some silver spoons, and a number of tubs and cauldrons. But most interesting of all were the personal possessions of the dead king—his helmet; his sword, gold hilted and decorated with garnets; his heavy six-inch long gold buckle, which may have held his sword belt; a pair of wonderful gold shoulder clasps for his cloak, set with garnets and stones of blue and white; and the gold frame of a purse, similarly inlaid and decorated with ornamental plaques, and the coins which it had contained.

The later Saxons were by no means isolated from the rest of Europe, and although they spent so much time fighting among themselves, and later against the Danes, there were many learned men among them, some of whom made the long and difficult journey to Rome. It was one of these, Alcuin from York, who was persuaded by Charlemagne (or Charles the Great), who became king of the countries we now call Germany, France and Lombardy, to join his court and educate his family. Later Alcuin became Abbot of Tours and founded a very famous school there.

In A.D. 800 Charlemagne went to Rome, and on Christmas Day the Pope placed the crown of the emperors of the old Roman Empire on his head, and hailed him as emperor of a revived 'Holy Roman Empire'.

We are told that Charlemagne, who was very tall and dignified, usually dressed quite simply in the clothes of his time. But for state occasions he dressed almost exactly as the Byzantine emperors did at that time, in a long tunic with tight sleeves bordered with gold and, over it, the wide-sleeved dalmatica of white silk or linen, with a heavy border of scarlet and gold and a gold and jewelled girdle supporting the sword of state. Over his shoulders he wore the paludamentum, made of very rich brocade manufactured for him at Constantinople, and the lorum (the civilian pallium) of cloth of gold brocaded in squares, with a ruby or an emerald in each square. Gloves, embroidered on the back in gold and set with precious stones, were also part of the regalia of Charlemagne and the later emperors of the Holy Roman Empire.

Gloves, of fine leather or silk, and richly decorated on the backs, are often mentioned in ancient German and Scandinavian stories as being possessed by kings and great lords. They were

Charlemagne

part of ceremonial costume, but were not in everyday use. Only the upper classes were privileged to wear real gloves at all, and peasants, if they needed something to protect their hands when they were doing certain kinds of hard work, were forbidden to wear any gloves other than fingerless ones.

Gloves often played a part in legal and other actions. A feudal

THE CLOTHES OF THE 'BARBARIANS'

lord would give a glove to his vassal as a sign of his authority over him—though, on the other hand, vassals often had to give gloves to their overlords as a sign of submission. When a king sent someone on a journey to do some important business for him he would give him a staff with his glove attached to it, to show that he represented the king, and when Charlemagne conferred upon a town the right to hold a market, he sent the townsmen his glove.

All kinds of rules and even superstitions became associated with gloves. For instance, when a knight wanted to challenge another he struck him with his glove if he could, or threw his glove down on the ground. When a fight was arranged, each party gave his glove as a pledge that he would attend and fight. Judges were not allowed to wear gloves when performing their duties, and no one might appear before the king in gloves, or take anything from another when wearing gloves, or offer a gloved hand to another. The reason for some of these rules was probably that the gloves of the time were very loose, and could be used to conceal a knife or other weapon, and by appearing with bare hands a man showed that he was not secretly armed.

Learned monks were not the only Saxons who visited other parts of Europe. One of the kings of Wessex, before his accession, spent some time at Charlemagne's court, and went with him to Rome in A.D. 800. King Alfred, too, was taken to Rome when he was quite a child. So some at least of the Saxons knew all about the grandeur of court dress and on state occasions their kings appear to have worn ankle-length tunics and large cloaks as other European kings did.

Charlemagne sent two silk tunics as a present to a British king, and Ethelred II, when he granted certain trading rights to a group of German merchants, demanded five pairs of gloves in return. So some at least of the Saxon kings were interested in fine clothes.

Saxon men did not cut their hair short, but they appear to have given it a good deal of attention, since we read, rather surprisingly, that King Alfred gave his father confessor some silver curling-tongs as a present.

96

THE CLOTHES OF THE 'BARBARIANS'

The clothes worn by the Normans who conquered England in 1066 were similar to those worn by the Saxons, and other races of northern Europe. The famous Bayeux tapestry, which is a record in embroidered pictures (not really in tapestry) of the Norman Conquest, shows the kings, Edward, Harold and William, all wearing ankle-length robes and big cloaks when enthroned and on important occasions. But both Harold and William, like the other Saxons and Normans, are shown wearing knee-length, long-sleeved tunics (probably over a sleeveless under-tunic, or shirt, short breeches and hose) with a short cloak fastened on the right shoulder.

A king from the
Bayeux Tapestry

Saxon from the
Bayeux Tapestry

Bishops and priests are shown wearing exactly the same clothes as other men, except in the case of Archbishop Stigand who, when officiating at the Coronation of Harold, is wearing the alb, chasuble and pallium.

The Saxons are distinguished from the Normans by being shown with moustaches and with their hair nearly to their shoulders, while the Normans are clean-shaven and have the backs of their necks and heads shaved quite high up.

In the battle the knights on both sides are wearing shirts of mail made of iron rings linked together. These have short legs

G   97

reaching just below the knee, and hoods which are worn over the head under the helmet. The helmets rise to a point at the top, and have straight pieces in front to protect the wearer's nose. Some of the most important people, such as William himself, are shown wearing chain mail over the lower leg as well, but most of them appear to have strips of cloth wrapped round and round the leg from ankle to knee, like puttees.

Knight from the
Bayeux Tapestry

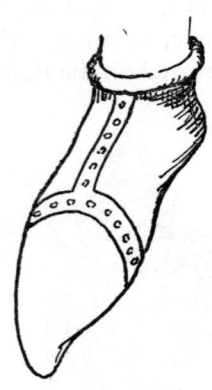

Norman shoe from
the Bayeux Tapestry

All the Normans and most of the Saxons carry long shields rounded at the top and pointed at the bottom, but a few Saxons are shown carrying the round shield which, by that time, was rather old-fashioned.

Norman women dressed very much as Saxon women did, in a long-sleeved under-tunic, the Saxon smock, which they called a chemise, and a short-sleeved over-tunic, or gown. Norman men, too, in pictures other than the Bayeux tapestry, are sometimes shown wearing a short-sleeved tunic over a long-sleeved one, often ankle length.

CHAPTER 11

In the Twelfth and Thirteenth Centuries

So far, all through the centuries, clothes had not changed very much in shape. They had only altered in detail—being longer or shorter, narrower or wider, loose or belted —at different times and in different places. And everywhere wealthy people had worn expensive fabrics such as silk, velvet, brocade and fine linen, often elaborately embroidered, while the poorest people wore home-spun cloth made from wool, flax, hemp, goat's or camel's hair, or whatever came to hand.

But towards the end of the eleventh century and during the twelfth there was, for a time, a slight change. After wearing straight loose garments for centuries, women took to drawing their dresses closely round their bodies by lacing them up tightly at the sides or back. At the same time they wore sleeves which were fairly narrow at the shoulder but which widened out so that the lower edge hung down several feet.

Or the sleeves might be tight fitting all the way to the wrist, but have a kind of cuff added which was so long that it trailed on the ground. Sometimes this band of material was tied in a great knot so that the wearer should not trip over it. Girdles were also long, with tassels and jewels on the ends which often reached to the bottom of the dress or to the floor. The dresses themselves were made very long, so that they trailed on the floor, and even had trains dragging behind.

Instead of fastening their long, semi-circular cloaks with a single brooch, women began to wear two brooches or clasps, one on each side of the cloak, with a cord or chain between.

But an even more surprising change was that in the twelfth century women discarded their head coverings and for the first

99

time for generations they showed their hair. They parted it in the centre and wore it in two plaits. Sometimes they twisted coloured ribbons in the plaits, and often they put little tapering cases made of silk, or of silver or gold, over the ends of the plaits to make them appear longer, or even wore false plaits.

Men, too, during the twelfth century, wore their hair long,

A mid-twelfth century woman

and arranged it in curls over the ears, forehead and shoulders. They made their cloth or soft leather shoes rather pointed at the toe, and wore hats without brims, with points or even spikes at the top of the crown.

Instead of long loose trousers they wore short breeches (either like present-day bathing trunks or like modern shorts) and long close-fitting hose or stockings, which reached well up the thighs and were tied by means of cords to the belt which held the breeches in place. The legs of the breeches were tucked into the top of the hose. Sometimes the hose seem to have had feet attached—like our socks and stockings—and sometimes not. Otherwise men's clothes did not change very much.

Close-fitting gowns for women did not stay in fashion for very long, and by the end of the twelfth century women had given them up. During the thirteenth century they wore loose full gowns again, pouched over a belt at the waist. And they rolled up their plaits over their ears, or at the backs of their heads and tucked them into net bags, sometimes of gold, which were called crespins. From about 1190 they began to wear a type of veil, called a wimple, which was drawn up under the chin, or just over the chin, and fastened on the top of the head, thus covering the front of the neck and the chest. Instead of the wimple some women placed a straight strip of linen under the chin and up to the top of the head, leaving the neck bare. This was called a barbette, and Queen Eleanor, the wife of Henry II (1154-89) is said to have introduced it into England.

A thirteenth century woman

When wearing the wimple or the barbette, both of which, in one form or another, remained popular for generations, women often wore a fillet, or band of stiff linen or similar material, like a crown, on their heads. Sometimes the top edge was cut in points, and sometimes the top was filled in so that the fillet became a kind of pill-box shaped hat. Or they wore a veil over their heads.

During the twelfth century many kings, nobles and knights from all over Europe went to Palestine with their followers to try to win back the Holy Places from the Saracens who had captured them. From about 1210 onwards they are shown in ancient sculptures and pictures wearing loose T-shaped tunics over their chain armour, or else straight strips of material with a hole for

Woman in a wimple   Woman wearing a barbette

the head to go through, which hung down back and front. Some writers have suggested that the tunics, or surcoats as they were called, were worn to prevent the fierce rays of the eastern sun from beating on the metal of the armour and making it unbearably hot. Whether this was so or not, the wearing of the surcoat over armour was followed by the introduction, when the Crusaders returned, of a new, long over-tunic which was also called a surcoat. It was worn by both men and women all through the thirteenth and fourteenth centuries, and, by women, in the fifteenth century. It covered the chest and back, but was open at the sides as far as the waist, though it was joined up from waist to hem.

Sometimes the armhole of the tunic worn under the surcoat was made very wide and loose, so that it filled up the space in the side of the surcoat. Sometimes the surcoat, although it was still open at the sides, was fitted with sleeves. When the wearer wished he or she could draw his arms out of the sleeves and leave them hanging loose.

Towards the end of the thirteenth century men began to wear a warm coat or gown out of doors instead of a cloak. It was still the familiar T-shape with an opening for the head and a short

Man wearing a surcoat   A long-sleeved coat

slit down the front, but the sleeves were made very long, so that they sometimes reached to the hem of the gown. But in the side of the sleeves was a slit through which the hand and arm could be thrust when necessary, leaving the sleeve hanging. The gown often had a collar of fur and a hood, also perhaps lined with fur, was sometimes attached to it. Often the whole gown, like the cloaks, was fur lined. This kind of gown was worn a great deal by doctors, architects and people of that kind. Another similar kind of gown had no real sleeves, but the upper part widened out from the shoulders to form capes over each arm.

Fur was used a great deal to line or trim all garments. Poorer people used sheep skin, rabbit, squirrel or other furs which they could get easily, but richer people liked to use those that were rarer and more beautiful. Few houses had glass in the windows, and the halls and rooms in which most people lived, with their fires burning in the centre, must have been very draughty. So it is not surprising that the people of northern Europe wore fur and warm woollen cloth when they could. But people also liked furs for their appearance. During the Crusades, Richard I of England and Philip II of France forbade their knights to wear expensive furs such as sable and ermine, but this order, like others of the same kind, does not seem to have had much effect. Whenever a Christian army was defeated the Saracens were sure of a rich spoil in fine furs.

In London a law was passed which 'provided and commanded that no woman of the city shall from henceforth go to market or in the king's highway, out of her house, with a hood furred other than with lamb skin or rabbit skin, on pain of losing her hood to the use of the Sheriffs'.

We wonder whether the women of London took any notice of this order and, if not, how many lost their hoods.

Hoods were often attached to garments, but they were also used alone. They were the most popular kind of head-dress for men for about two hundred years. A very popular kind of hood was like the knitted Balaclava helmet that many boys and men still wear in very cold weather, and which soldiers and sailors wore during the war. It covered the head, ears and neck, and had a 'gorget' or wide cape-like section to cover the shoulders. But the hood of the thirteenth century had a point sticking out at the back of the head, and towards the end of the century this point grew longer and longer, until at last men added a pipe or tail of material to it, which hung three or four feet down the wearer's back. They called the tail a 'liripipe'.

Coifs, which were like close-fitting bonnets tied under the chin, also probably originated with the Crusaders. They wore them under their chain helmets. But they became popular for everyday wear by men, and were of white linen. Hats with low crowns and wide brims were sometimes worn on top of the coif or hood, especially by travellers. They often had cords attached to each side so that the hat could be slung over the back if not wanted.

Man in a coif

Hood with gorget and liripipe

The twelfth century also saw the beginnings of heraldry. Knights who were clothed from head to foot in mail must all have looked very much alike and been very difficult to recognize, especially after they began to wear a barrel-shaped helmet which covered their faces. So they began to put simple emblems or signs on their shields and on a little flag or pennon which they attached to their spears, so that their friends and followers would know one knight from another.

At first each man chose any sign he liked. He might simply have a coloured stripe painted across his shield, or he might have a cross or star, or a picture of an animal or bird, or some other easily recognized object painted on it. Some men used emblems that suggested their own names. Sir Roger de Trumpington, for instance, whose effigy can be seen on a brass in Trumpington Church near Cambridge, used a device of trumpets and crosses, and a knight with the name of Windigate used a drawing of a portcullis—which is certainly a gate through which the wind blows.

At first each man had his own sign, and fathers and sons, if they were fighting in the same war or taking part in the same tournament, might have different emblems. But before long men began to use their emblems on the seals with which they sealed legal documents, and on the gateways of their castles and on their other possessions. Many people in the twelfth and thirteenth centuries could not read, but they could recognize an emblem and learn who the man was who used it. Soon knights realized that it was convenient for sons to use the same signs as their father, but with some slight difference, such as a different colour, or the addition of some small further sign. And on the death of the father the eldest son took over the father's emblems, whilst younger sons used similar but slightly different designs.

After a time knights had their emblems painted on the surcoat which they wore over their coats of mail, and the designs themselves came, in time, to be called 'coats of arms'. Before long emblems and coats of arms became part of everyday life and of normal clothing.

Another result of the Crusades was that men from all over Europe came in contact—some of them for the first time—with the rich colours and gorgeous fabrics of southern and eastern Europe. Many of them wanted to be able to buy similar lovely things for themselves and their families. Soon beautiful silken materials, sometimes interwoven with gold threads, began to find their way more freely than before into northern and western Europe, including Britain. They were called by strange and charming names, which were sometimes derived from the places they came from (or which people thought they came from) such as damask (from Damascus), gauze (probably from Gaza), baldekyn (from the Italian name for Baghdad), and so on. Other names for silken fabrics were samite, sarcinet and cendal. A mixture of wool and silk was called camlet because it had originally been made from camel's hair and silk. Some of these names have survived and we still use them (though not always for silken materials) but many have died out.

Silken fabrics, as well as jewels, scents, spices and innumerable other things, were sent across Europe by merchants from Venice, the greatest and wealthiest trading city in Europe. Their pack horses and galleys carried luxuries from the east to the cities and ports in the north and west, afterwards returning to their owners laden with linen from Germany, furs from Scandinavia, cloth from Flanders and wool from England. Cotton materials, too, began to find their way from Egypt and farther east, through Venice, or from Spain, which had been overrun by the Moors. A material called fustian was made with a linen warp and a cotton woof.

Of course, the rich expensive fabrics could only be worn by the wealthy, and most people still made their simple tunics and gowns from their own home-spun linen and woollen fabrics. Nevertheless, trade was making it necessary for fabrics to be manufactured in far larger quantities. Spinning and weaving developed into businesses carried on by men and women who did it for a living and not only to make cloth for their own and their family's use. Certain countries gradually became famous for certain fabrics—Germany for linen, for instance, and Flanders for woollen cloth. The very best wool in Europe was that which grew on the backs of English sheep, and even before the Norman Conquest merchants came from as far away as Italy to buy wool direct from English monasteries and farms.

In the twelfth and thirteenth centuries English weavers wove cloth for use in England, but did not sell very much abroad. But English wool merchants exported a great deal of raw wool to Europe, chiefly to Flanders. The Flemings spun it into thread and wove it into fine cloth, some of which they sold back to the English.

The making of garments, too, began to be a specialized business. The simple straight or T-shaped tunic in linen or wool, and the rectangular or semi-circular cloak, could be made by the woman who had woven the cloth. But as clothes became more complicated, as they were soon to do, and when they were made from cloth which had come from abroad and cost a great deal of money, they had to be made by experts. The first charter to a Guild of tailors appears to have been granted in Hamburg in Germany in 1152.

Shoemakers also began to form themselves into guilds or companies early in the twelfth century. Shoemakers were called cordovanners, or cordwainers, because the leather from which the best shoes were made came from Cordova in Spain. It was the skin of a certain kind of goat.

Cordwainer's knife

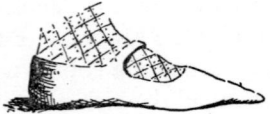

Late thirteenth century
shoe

In England there was a Cordwainers' Guild as early as the reign of Henry I (1100-35). When the London company was formed is not certain, but it was probably in the thirteenth century. On their arms are three goats' heads. Other companies show on their arms shoes, sandals, clogs, or pictures of Sts. Crispin and Crispianus in the cauldron, or standing holding palm leaves to show they were martyrs. Quite often the knives and other tools used by shoemakers, especially an almost semi-circular knife which seems to have been used from the very earliest times right up to the present, appear on the arms.

October 25th, St. Crispin's day, was celebrated as a holiday by shoemakers' guilds. Processions including some people dressed as Crispin, Ursula and other persons mentioned in the legends passed through the streets. Members of the London company each wearing a new gown assembled in their hall, went in procession to church, and then sat down to a banquet.

By the middle of the twelfth century the tanners had been forbidden to live in the forests and ordered to live in towns, perhaps so that the authorities could keep an eye on them. Certain towns which were near the oak forests in time became famous for shoes and other leather work. Northampton was one of them, and King John had a pair of riding boots made for him by a Northampton craftsman. All the work from beginning to end was done by the one man and the price was ninepence.

In most towns the tanners and the different people connected with leather selling and shoemaking were, at first, members of the same guilds, but there were quarrels from time to time, especially between the cordwainers, or shoe-*makers*, and the cobblers, or shoe-*menders*, and in time they usually separated into different companies.

Fourteenth century patten

Patten-making was also a very important trade for centuries. Pattens had thick wooden soles with leather straps to attach them to the foot, and were shaped in such a way that they raised the wearer several inches from the muddy ground so that he or she could walk through puddles without getting his or her cloth or leather shoes wet and muddy. Sometimes the wooden sole had a round metal stand under it instead of the wooden supports.

People who could afford it not only wore fine fabrics but also precious stones, not only because of their beauty and value but because of the belief that such stones had magic powers—that they could protect the wearer from danger, heal him if he were sick, and give him certain good qualities.

For instance, people believed that diamonds could protect them from their enemies; that emeralds would make them prosperous and protect their eyes; that rubies would give them peace of mind, make them serene and content and save them from poverty; that sapphires would give them heavenly happiness; that chalcedony would give them power and health; that amethysts would save them from the bad effects of drinking too much; that coral was a remedy for bleeding—and so on.

These beliefs had survived from heathen times. In Ancient Greece and Rome certain stones were believed to be connected with certain planets and with the seasons, and each month had its own lucky stone. Anyone who could wore jacinths in January, amethysts in February, jaspers in March, sapphires in April, agates or emeralds in May, emeralds or chalcedony in June, onyx or cornelian in July, cornelian or sardonyx in August, chrysolite in September, beryl or aquamarine in October, topaz in November, and ruby, chrysoprase, turquoise or malachite in December. These superstitions have survived to some extent even to the present day, and people still sometimes wear their 'birthstones' according to which month they were born in.

Girdles set with precious stones were believed to be especially valuable, and we read of men wearing golden girdles set with over fifty precious stones, in the belief that they would ensure them happiness, health, honour and safety. These girdles were very valuable indeed, and a German ruler in the twelfth century bought a whole manor, or estate, and paid for it with a gold girdle set with pearls.

The demand for jewels was so great that there were not enough to go round. Even as early as the first century A.D. there were men in Italy who were skilful at making artificial gems, especially pearls, and at making cheaper metals look like gold. By the thirteenth century it was necessary to make laws against the sale of imitation jewellery—but a great deal must have been used all the same, either with or without the knowledge of the wearer.

When the grave of King Edward I of England, who died in 1307, was opened it was discovered that the 'gold' used in his elaborate clothes was only base-metal gilded, and the pearls and other gems were artificial. But this does not prove that he wore anything but genuine jewels when he was alive.

The gloves worn by kings on state occasions and by higher church dignitaries were often jewelled on the backs and on the gauntlets. Such jewelled gloves were found in the tombs both

IN THE TWELFTH AND THIRTEENTH CENTURIES
of King John and King Edward I of England, and they are often shown on effigies and in pictures of kings in illuminated manuscripts.

The gloves which kings and great lords wore on ordinary occasions, even when not actually jewelled, were of expensive material and were richly embroidered. When Richard I of England was on his way home from the Crusades he tried to slip through the country of his enemy the Duke of Austria, but he was recognized and captured because someone noticed his fine and expensive gloves, which could only have belonged to a person of importance.

By this time, the late twelfth century, the wearing of gloves was gradually becoming more general. Women began to wear them for the first time. Glove-making, like tailoring, was becoming a trade at which many people earned their livings.

CHAPTER 12

Clothes are Made to Fit

For hundreds and hundreds of years, as we have seen, clothes had almost always been made from pieces of fabric woven or cut into simple geometrical shapes—rectangles, squares, circles, semi-circles and so on—folded or draped round the wearers with very little shaping and few seams. But with the fourteenth century there came the beginnings of a real change.

At first the only difference was that men's tunics and women's gowns were made a little narrower and therefore closer fitting. But by 1350 the general appearance of the garments had changed completely. The bodices of both men's and women's clothes were shaped and fitted to their wearers as they had never been before (except perhaps in ancient Crete). They were made to fit, not by drawing them in with laces, but by cutting the fabric and making seams back and front as well as under the arms, and by inserting gussets (triangular pieces) where necessary.

At first the skirts of women's dresses (and of the long

Women of the fourteenth century

112

gowns which elderly and dignified men continued to wear) simply flared out from the waist, and shaped gores (tapering pieces of material) were put in to make them very wide at the hem. But towards the end of the century the skirt was gathered on to the bottom of the bodice, about at the hip line.

The effigy of Anne of Bohemia, the wife of King Richard II, in Westminster Abbey shows her wearing a gown of this kind. The long sleeves were buttoned closely from elbow to wrist. The girdle or belt was worn low down on the hips.

Men as well as women wore belts at hip level, and their bodices were often fastened all the way from neck to hips with buttons which almost touched one another. For people had at last discovered that very convenient and, to us, commonplace method of fastening garments together, the button and buttonhole. From this time onwards 'buttony', or making buttons, gradually became an important industry at which many people earned their livings. The people of certain villages would make buttons of certain traditional patterns.

Men usually wore two tunics. The under one, which was called a gipon, had tight sleeves and a straight, tight skirt joined to the bodice. As time went on the skirt became shorter and shorter until it reached only about half-way down the thigh. The outer tunic, or cotehardie, was similar to the gipon and was buttoned or laced over it as far as the hip belt, below which the skirt was fuller than that of the gipon and was, at first, open in front, though later it was buttoned all the way down. The sleeve of the outer tunic often fitted as far as the elbow and then widened out into a point or flap.

The hose, or stockings, which men wore were separate, one for each leg, until about 1380, when they were attached to one another and became more like present-day tights, or pants. They were often of very bright colours, and one leg might be of one colour and the other of another, or one leg might be striped and the other plain. Sometimes the two sides of one leg might be of different colours and the two sides of one doublet.

Fashionable men in Germany in the fourteenth century were in the habit of decorating themselves with little bells. The mantle

H

which one of the German emperors wore at his coronation was trimmed with three hundred and fifty-five little gold bells shaped like pomegranates, and another German wore a costume decorated with five hundred bells. This fashion spread to other countries. Bells were put round the hems of garments, round the edges of hoods, on the ends of liripipes, on the points of shoes and along the edge of the baldric, which was a decorated band

Men of the fourteenth century

of material that was sometimes worn over one shoulder and under the other arm. There was even a proverb which said 'The tinkle of bells the gentleman spells.'

Preachers such as Wyclif protested indignantly against the fashion for wearing bells, and some governors tried to stop it, too, but without effect. The city of Nuremberg decreed firmly that 'no persons shall wear any bell, large or small, nor any bauble of silver attached on chains to their girdles'—but bells were still in use more than a hundred years later.

Both men and women, at first, still wore the long surcoat with the open sides, but men gradually gave it up. As time went on the top part of the women's surcoat became narrower and narrower, until it was a strip only a few inches wide at front and back, sometimes of fur, or else edged with fur. The opening at the side became deeper and deeper, so that the side of the tight-fitting under-dress was visible to below the belt, which encircled the hips. In the front of the skirt part of the surcoat, and of other long gowns, there were sometimes two slits, through which the wearer could put his or her hands in order to reach the pouch or keys which hung on the belt. There were still no pockets as we know them, and the pouch or purse which both men and women wore attached to their belts was a very necessary and important possession. It was envelope shaped, and the flap of the man's pouch often had slots cut into it through which a dagger fitted.

Both men's and women's garments were cut low at the neck at this time, and as many women had given up wearing wimples, their necks, throats and chests, like those of men, were bare. Men still wore the caped hood when they went out. The liripipe became longer and longer. When men wore the hoods in the normal way the liripipe hung down their backs. Sometimes a hat was worn on top of the hood. But sometimes—perhaps, at first, in warm weather—men took to placing the face-opening of the hood over their heads with the gorget or shoulder cape hanging down over one shoulder and the liripipe over the other. Then they took the liripipe and twisted it round their heads like a turban so that the end of the gorget stuck up like a cock's comb. Even after it had been twisted round the head the liripipe was sometimes so long that men hung it over their arms so that it should not trail on the ground.

During the fourteenth century men liked to have the edges of all their garments cut into jagged points or scallops. This dagging, as it was called, appeared at the bottom edges of tunics and round the gorgets of hoods, all the way round the edges of cloaks and, in fact, anywhere where it was possible to introduce it. Even the surcoats worn over armour were sometimes dagged and an Englishman named Sir John Chandos is said to have lost his life in battle because he fell over the points of his surcoat and was killed before he could get up.

A 'Paul's window' shoe

Even the soft, close-fitting boots which men wore when they were riding or taking part in some outdoor activity, were often dagged at the tops. Shoes were often of silk or velvet or, of course, of leather, and were decorated with embroidery or jewels. In *The Canterbury Tales* Chaucer speaks of his Parish Clerk having 'Paul's Window carven on his shoe'—by which he meant a rose shape, similar to the rose-window in Old St. Paul's in London. An ancient wall-painting of the time showed men wearing shoes decorated in this way.

Women did not wear garments with dagged edges so much as men did—neither did they as a rule wear the liripipe. But so that they too should have something long and dangling they wore 'tippets' which were narrow bands of fabric attached to the wearer's arm just above the elbow and hanging down almost to the floor.

There was a great deal of distress all over Europe during the fourteenth century. The terrible plague which people called the Black Death carried off a very large number of men and women, and afterwards, in England and other countries, there was discontent among the working people, with rioting and rebellion. But at the same time many people (such as those, in England, who kept large numbers of sheep, or who were merchants dealing with wool) were more prosperous than they had ever been before.

In England, too, far more cloth was being woven. In order to help English weavers, merchants were forbidden to bring foreign cloth into the country, and clever Flemish weavers were encouraged to settle in England to teach English weavers their secrets.

English cloth merchants bought the raw wool from the sheep farmers and passed it on to the village women who spun it into thread. Then they collected the thread and passed it on to the weavers, who wove it on looms in their own homes. The woven cloth was then passed on to the fullers. By this time the fulling, which had before always been done by hand, was more often done in fulling mills built by rivers. The running water turned wheels which worked great hammers which beat the cloth as it was washed, to shrink and felt it. The Flemish weavers may have taught the English how to build fulling mills.

When the cloth was dry it was stretched on frames and the surface was shorn, or cropped, by highly skilled men using huge shears or scissors about four feet long.

The merchants took the finished cloth to the ports, from which it was carried to foreign lands. As time went on more and more cloth was sold abroad, and less and less raw wool. This did not please the wool merchants very much, but English cloth became very famous and many English cloth merchants became very wealthy.

Although they did not belong to the nobility, such people as sheep farmers and wool and cloth merchants began to spend their money on fine fabrics, jewels and furs. But in the Middle Ages it was thought very important that a man's position in the world, his class, should be obvious from his dress. So laws were passed in many countries laying down strict rules as to what could or could not be worn by different people.

In England, for instance, according to a law passed in 1363, only members of the royal family and the wealthier nobles were to wear ermine, or pearls anywhere except on head-dresses. The common people, below the rank of squire or knight, were forbidden to wear silk and were ordered to wear woollen fabrics only, without jewellery or embroidery. Squires and knights with incomes below a certain amount were allowed to wear cloth of silver and silver girdles if they wished, but wealthier knights and their ladies might wear cloth of gold, gowns embroidered and trimmed with gems, and expensive furs.

It seems to have been very difficult to enforce these laws and people do not seem to have taken much notice of them.

Not that all the sensible middle-class people of the time wanted to deck themselves out in costly fashionable clothes. Most of them, probably, were quiet, sober, hard-working men and women who wore clothes of good quality which were not particularly striking or up-to-date. About this time, the middle of the fourteenth century, some of the trade guilds began to arrange for their members to wear special clothes—or, rather, clothes of certain colours and made of some particular cloth. In shape they would be similar to the ordinary everyday clothes of the time. The grocers, for instance, at one time wore scarlet and green, the haberdashers white and blue, the fishmongers blue, and so on. The wardens bought the costumes and the members paid for them, and before long the various guilds began to attach great importance to correct dress at their meetings and ceremonies. They laid down rules too as to what their apprentices should wear.

Clothes worn by people who were not wealthy often had to last a lifetime, and were passed on from father to son and from mother to daughter, as we know from wills that have survived —so they could not possibly have been in the latest fashion. Many elderly people, and younger ones who lived quiet industrious lives, probably continued to wear the clothes fashionable a generation earlier.

A book has survived since 1394 which was written by a well-to-do elderly Frenchman for the instruction of his fifteen-year-old wife. In it there are several references to clothes, and the writer makes it very clear that he is more anxious that his wife shall be neat in her dress than that she shall be up-to-date. The low-necked gowns and unveiled heads and necks of the fashionable world were not for her.

'Have a care that you be honestly clad, without new devices and without too much or too little frippery,' he writes. '. . . take care that the collar of your shift and of your cotte (gown) and surcotte do not hang out one over the other, as happens with certain drunken, foolish or witless women who have no care for their honour, nor for the honesty of their estate or of their husbands and who walk with roving eyes . . . their hair straggling out of their wimples and the collars of their shifts and cottes crumpled the one upon the other. . . . Have a care that your hair, wimple, kerchief and hood, and all the rest of your attire be well arranged and decently ordered, that none who see you can laugh or mock at you, but that all the others may find in you an example of fair and simple and decent array.'

In another part of the book he gives her instructions about looking after their clothes and furs and keeping them clean and free from moths. He gives her several recipes for removing stains and grease spots, though he does not seem certain that some of them will work. He speaks of the tailors, furriers and shoemakers they will be employing from time to time to make clothes and shoes for them, and he knows where the best cloth and other materials are to be found and how much they should cost.

Many fourteenth-century women wore their hair plaited and twisted round their heads in various ways, and, like this young French wife, still wore a veil or kerchief over it, and possibly a

Fourteenth century head-dresses

wimple. But fashionable women sometimes wore little caps of network, sometimes of gold and set with jewels, or they tucked their plaits up in various ways in cages or frames made of gold or gilded wire. Sometimes the cages were like two half-cylinders, one in front of each ear. Sometimes they were semi-circular or horse-shoe shaped and encircled the wearer's forehead and face to below her ears. Some women, instead of wearing a wire frame round their faces, wore a head-dress made up of a large number of little frills of material along the front edge of a semi-circle of linen, and others surrounded their faces with something that looked like a little padded bolster.

But it was towards the end of the fourteenth century and during the fifteenth that some of the most extraordinary head-dresses ever known in Europe were worn by women. One was called the henin, and is said to have been first worn by a Queen

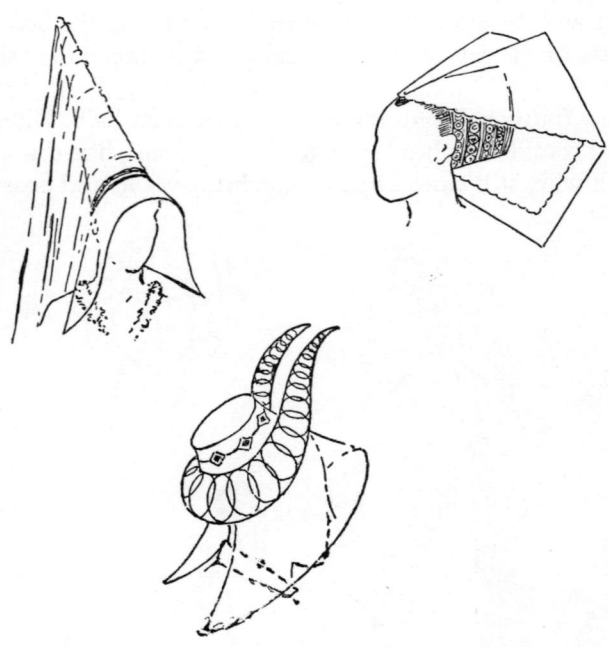

Late fourteenth and fifteenth century heads

Isabella of France. It was introduced into England by Anne of Bohemia, who married King Richard II in 1383. It was a long, tapering, sugar-loaf or dunce's cap shape, with a veil hanging from it. It was popular for nearly a hundred years, but during that time it was only one of many very fantastic head-dresses of all shapes and sizes. Some were like lofty flower-pots; some had great horns sticking out at the sides and were very wide; some were a development of the bolster shape which had formerly framed the face, but which now became a huge padded circle, like a lifebelt, which might be as much as two yards round. It was bent into all kinds of shapes and put over a netted cage which enclosed the hair.

Sometimes veils were worn over these strange head-dresses, and sometimes not. But one thing was essential—not a scrap of hair must be visible. Women even plucked out the hairs at the backs of their necks and on their foreheads so that they should not show.

Head-dresses, hats, and the fabrics for making them often came from Milan in Italy, and were called 'Millayne'. Our word millinery comes from this fourteenth-century word.

Men's hats were almost as striking as those worn by women. Huge hats of beaver or velvet were popular, also all kinds of fantastic turbans made with hoods and liripipes. While women hid their hair completely, fashionable men wore theirs long and curly.

During the 1380s men and women began to wear a gown that was a complete contrast to those with a tight-fitting bodice. In a way, it was not unlike the paenula, or circular cloak, of the Romans, except that pieces were cut out from the circle at each side and the seams joined so that the garment had long pointed sleeves. It was called a houppelande, and was often ankle or ground length.

Sometimes the houppelande was open down the front, but more often closed, with an opening for the head to go through. A rather wide belt held it in place at the waist. The necks of men's houppelandes were often very high, reaching up even to the ears, but those worn by women at this time were often cut quite low in the neck. Houppelandes were often very bulky and were made of thick heavy material. Sometimes the wide skirts were as much as twelve yeards round the hem.

The full, heavy skirt was sometimes slit up the front or sides or both, and sometimes the huge sleeves were gathered into a cuff, which might be of fur. When the sleeves hung down they were often edged or lined with fur. At this time big, bag-shaped or bell-shaped sleeves were often worn with the short tight tunics and coats as well as with the houppelande, for both types of garment were fashionable at the same time.

Houppelandes

CHAPTER 13

Sleeves, Hats and Pointed Toes

After men and women began to wear shaped and fitted clothes, they seem to have racked their brains to think of new and strange ways of making their garments. For the next two or three hundred years clothes were cut into all kinds of fantastic and unheard of shapes and people seem to have

Fifteenth century man and woman

123

wanted to look like almost anything except natural men and women.

During the fifteenth century when, in England, the Wars of the Roses were being fought and sometimes a Lancastrian and sometimes a Yorkist king sat on the throne, styles began to change more quickly than they had ever done before.

Although men still wore both the long houppelande and the short tunic, the tunics gradually changed until, instead of being smooth and tight-fitting, they were shaped to the body by being gathered and pleated. The waists of men's garments were made as small as possible, but the sleeves, towards the end of the century, were gathered and padded so that the shoulders were very wide.

The sleeves were all kinds of shapes—wide and full all the way down and turned back over the wrist to show the coloured or fur lining, or padded and bunched at the shoulder but close fitting at the wrist, or very long and straight with a slit at the elbow for the arm to go through, or slit all the way down, but with a little cuff at the bottom through which men could thrust their hands when they wished. Quite often the sleeves were separate from the garments they were worn with, and were tied on at the shoulders with cords laced through holes, and the sleeves were sometimes stuffed until they looked like bolsters.

The skirt part of the tunics were made very full, but sometimes they were so short that they only reached a few inches below the waist. With the short doublet men often wore a very short cloak, only about waist length, fastened on one shoulder.

Fur linings and trimmings were still very popular, and a crowd of wealthy fifteenth-century men and women, dressed in their finest clothes, must have looked very gay indeed, as nearly all garments were covered with very large embroidered patterns and the hose were of bright colours. Men often used their family colours—those which appeared on their coats of arms—for their hose, one leg of one colour and one another. Dagging gradually went out of fashion.

The houppelande was often enormously wide and full, and must have been very heavy and hot to wear. A fifteenth-century

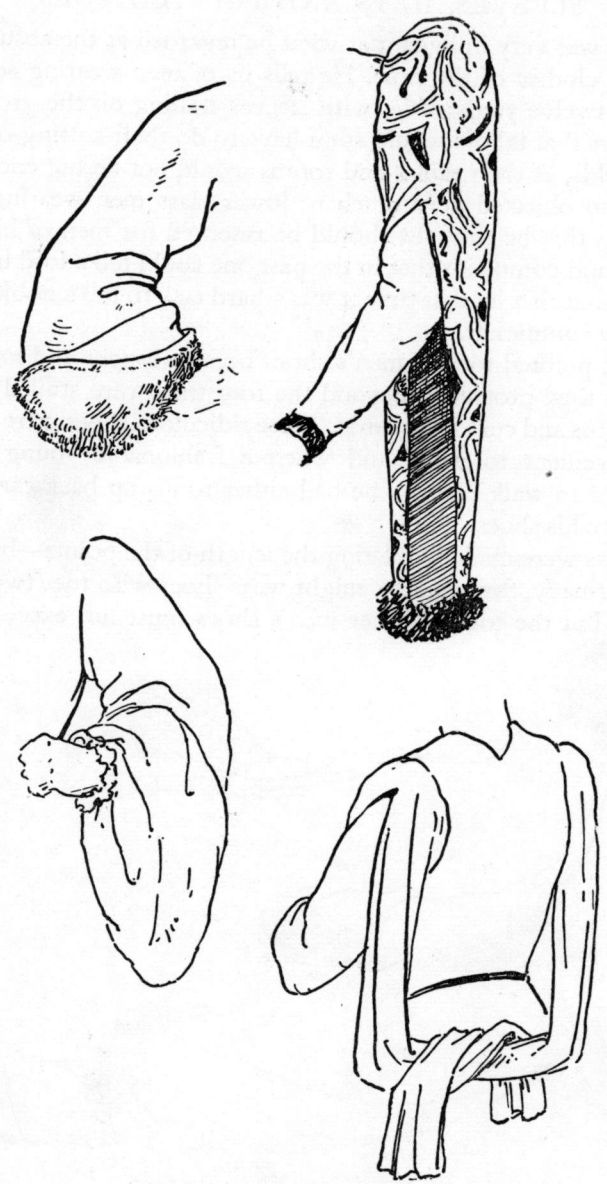

Fifteenth century sleeves

writer was very indignant at what he regarded as the absurdity of the clothes of the time. He tells us of men wearing scarlet robes twelve yards wide, with sleeves trailing on the ground. He says that tailors would soon have to do their cutting-out in the fields, as their tables and rooms would not be big enough. He also objected very much to lower class men wearing the clothes that he thought should be reserved for men of higher rank, and complains that in the past one could tell a lord by his array, but that by that time it was a hard task to tell a nobleman from a commoner.

The pointed toes of men's shoes became longer and longer. When they protruded beyond the foot they were stuffed with dry moss and curled upwards. These ridiculous shoes were most inconvenient to wear, and when a fashionable young man wanted to walk upstairs he had either to go up backwards or remove his shoes.

Laws were made regulating the length of the points—barons in Germany, for instance, might wear shoes with toes two feet long, but the toes of other men's shoes must not exceed one

Fifteenth century shoes and pattens

foot. In England toes more than two feet long could only be worn by men who had an income of more than £40 a year—which was quite a lot in those days. About 1420 the really fashionable dandy wore garters round his leg just below the knee, to which the long toes of his shoes were attached by gold or silver chains. This fashion is said to have been started by James I of Scotland, but in a portrait he is shown with the toes of his shoes attached not to a garter but to his waist girdle.

Long pointed pattens were sometimes worn with the turned-up shoes, and the two together were then called 'Devil's Claws'.

At least one shoemaker of the fifteenth century was as prosperous and successful as Dick Whittington, though his name is not so well known, and there are not so many stories about him. He was Sir Simon Eyre, and in Henry VI's time he became Lord Mayor of London, and built Leaden Hall as 'a market place kept every Monday for leather, where the shoemakers might buy of the tanners without seeking any further'.

Laws were made, too, about the height of the tapering head-dress worn by women—the henin. Women of rank might wear henins one yard high, but others must restrict theirs to twenty-four inches.

Men did not allow themselves to be outdone by the strange head-dresses worn by women in the fifteenth century. They, too, wore hats of a wide variety of shapes and sizes, and the hood placed over the head with the liripipe twisted round it like a kind of turban was still worn. But the liripipe was now often embroidered, and a stiffened roll of material was put round the edge of the original face opening of the hood (which was now put over the head) and formed a kind of brim.

Towards the end of the century men sometimes wore little close-fitting caps over their long hair, which hung down on to their shoulders. On top of the cap they sometimes put a wide-brimmed felt hat adorned with an immense bunch of feathers. The hat often hung down the wearer's back, or over his arm, supported by a scarf which was attached to it.

All kinds of strange things, such as acrostics, heraldic emblems, monograms and whole coats of arms were embroidered on the clothes of wealthy men and women. A French prince, Charles of Orleans, once wore a houppelande decorated with nine hundred and sixty pearls, and on one of its huge sleeves a whole love lyric was embroidered, complete with words and music. The bars of the music were of gold, and each note consisted of four pearls.

Charles, Duke of Burgundy, who was one of the richest and most powerful princes of the time, once wore a doublet of

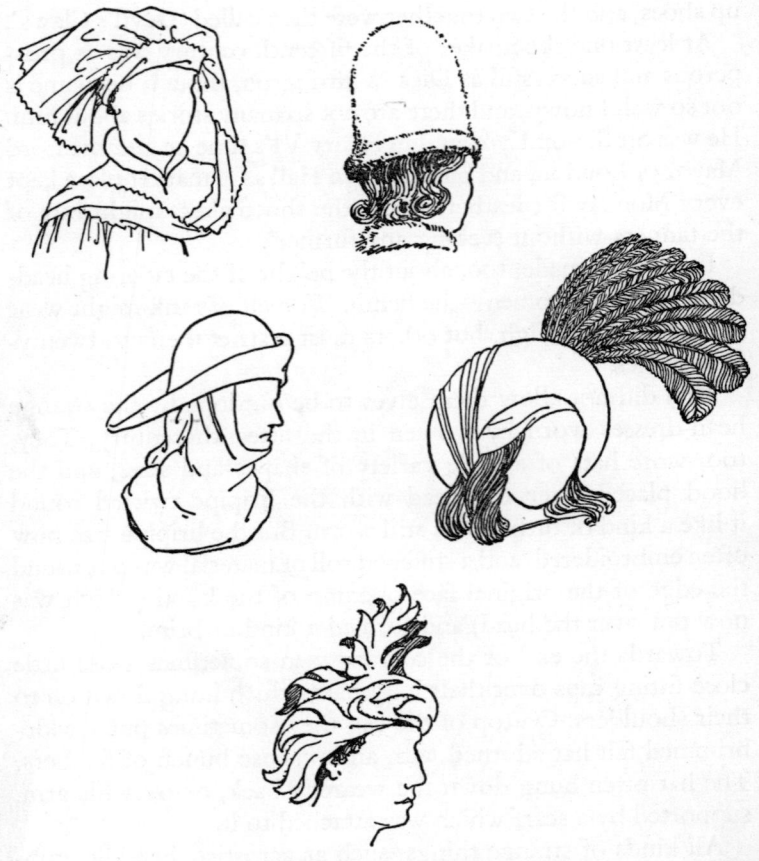

Fifteenth century men's hats

cherry-red velvet on the breast of which a large bear was embroidered in silver. The muzzle of the bear was of rubies and sapphires. Another day he wore a doublet of black velvet, on the left sleeve of which a spray of twenty-two roses was embroidered, each rose being made up of sapphires, rubies and pearls.

It was the Burgundian court that introduced a fashion which seemed very strange in those days of bright colours. It was the wearing of black by fashionable men. To keep up a constant supply of richly decorated and brightly coloured clothes must have cost an enormous amount of money and of trouble. So in the second half of the fifteenth century it was decreed that black velvet should become the official court dress of Burgundy. For the first time black clothes were looked upon as indicating refinement and correctness.

In time, and very gradually, the habit of wearing black spread. Now, centuries later, it is the custom for men all over Europe to wear black for formal occasions—but it all started at the Burgundian court in the fifteenth century at a time when no colours were too bright or gaudy, and no jewels, feathers, furs or fabrics too elaborate or costly for men of rank to wear, and men's clothes were usually more showy and fantastic than those of women—except, of course, for the head-dresses.

Women's clothes remained fairly simple. Their gowns were usually in the style of the houppelande, with a fairly wide belt rather high round the waist. In the latter part of the century the neck of the gown was often cut very low, in a V-shape, down to the waist and the space was filled in with a 'stomacher' of a different material. This fashion was popular with men, too.

Towards the end of the fifteenth century women gave up their strange head-dresses, which had completely hidden their hair, and began to let their hair hang freely down their backs. Sometimes they put a little net cap on their heads. But at the same time the head-dress shaped like the gable end of a roof, which you can see in the drawing, became very popular. It was worn by Elizabeth of York, the wife of the first Tudor king, Henry VII, but it remained in fashion for a long time. Catherine of Aragon, Henry VIII's first wife, wore it in the next century.

I

Not only did men's and women's heads change in appearance towards the end of the fifteenth century, but their feet also. The pointed shoe disappeared, and broad shoes with square toes took their place. They are said to have originated in Flanders about 1470.

As we have seen, people of wealth and nobility connected with royal courts found it necessary to have a great many outfits of different kinds, and to spend a fortune on them. The pictures in books and the effigies on tombs which have come down to us

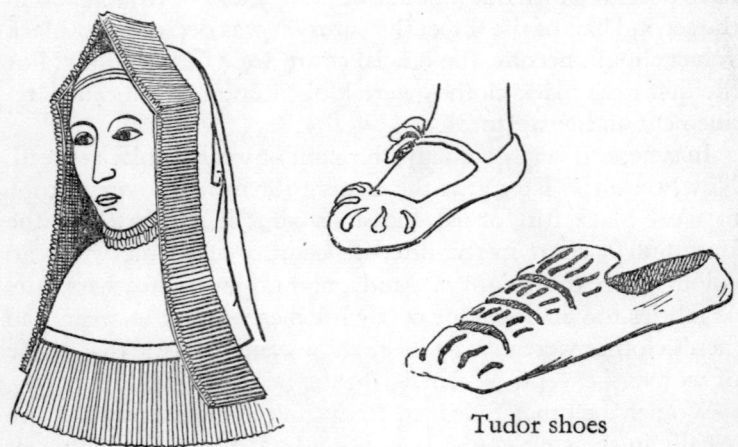

Tudor shoes

A gable-shaped head-dress

are very often of these wealthy people, and it is their clothes, too, which are so often described in contemporary accounts of great occasions. If we could go back to the fifteenth century we should still find that most people were dressed in simple, and often old-fashioned, clothes, and that elderly men and women were still wearing the clothes they had worn when they were young.

Cloth was expected to wear for many years. A fifteenth-century letter which has survived tells us that the writer has bought thirty-eight yards of green sarsenet (a silk material) and the London merchant from whom she has bought it has assured her that it will last her own and her child's life-time. We also read of a fifteenth-century ale-wife who has worn the same everyday clothes for forty years—by which time they can hardly have been in the height of fashion.

A fifteenth century peasant woman

All the same, there were probably a great many people who did try to copy the fashions worn by the rich and the great. Edward IV, like so many others before and after him, tried by law to compel his humbler subjects to dress simply and economically, and to stop imitating the nobility. For instance, fashionable men padded their clothes to make them the shape they wanted, and particularly to make the shoulders broad, and Edward IV's laws decreed that no man of the rank of yeoman or under should wear any such stuffings in his 'purpoint' or doublet, but a lining only. Men of lower rank than lords were forbidden to wear the very short doublets and cloaks that were fashionable, and tailors were forbidden to make them. The shoes of ordinary men were not to have points more than two inches long and cordwainers or cobblers in London and for three miles round were forbidden to make them under pain of cursing by the clergy, and a fine of twenty shillings.

No common labourer or servant or person in a similar class was to wear any garment made of cloth costing more than two shillings a yard, or hose costing more than fourteen pence a pair, and their wives must not wear coverchiefs, or head veils, costing more than twelve pence each. Neither of them was to have girdles garnished with silver. Wives of men with incomes of less than £40 a year were forbidden to pay more than ¾d. for their coverchiefs.

A few letters that have survived from the fifteenth century show us that the families of people higher in the social scale than labourers but of less exalted rank than kings and dukes sometimes had very few clothes indeed, and were anything but extravagant in buying them.

One of the finest collections of letters we have are those written by a Norfolk family called Paston between about 1430 and 1503. The Pastons owned houses and land but they and the people they associated with seem to have had very little ready money and often to have found it quite difficult to buy such a costly article as a new gown.

One of the early letters was written in 1440 by Agnes Paston to her husband, Sir William Paston, who was a judge and who was then in London. She writes that a young lady named Margaret Mauteby, who was going to marry their son John, has arrived at their house and that the two young people have met for the first time. But, the letter goes on, '. . . if you would buy her a gown, her mother would give thereto a goodly fur; the gown needeth for to be had; and of colour it would be a goodly blue, or else a bright sanguine'. By sanguine Agnes meant red.

It seems very odd that a girl whose parents, like the Pastons, were well-to-do landowners should need a gown so badly, and that her future father-in-law should be expected to buy it for her. But shopping was not easy in those days, and we constantly find in the letters that the men, on their visits to London, are being asked to buy cloth, gold or silk for embroidery, girdles, thread and so on.

Many women besides the Pastons must have been dependent on their men folk or on friends to buy them what they needed when they happened to travel to London or some other big town. For there were no shops of the kind we know. In country districts it must have been difficult to get anything but the very simplest things and those only in small quantities.

In April 1452, Margaret, who had by this time been married to John Paston for several years, wrote to tell him that Queen Margaret, the wife of Henry VI, had spent two days in the district, and in her letter Margaret Paston begged her husband to buy her 'something for my neck. When the Queen was here I

SLEEVES, HATS AND POINTED TOES

borrowed my cousin Elizabeth Clere's device, for I durst not for shame go with my beads amongst so many fresh gentlewomen as here were at that time.'

Perhaps the 'device' was something like the one in the drawing, and Margaret felt that her more simple beads were dreadfully old-fashioned. But she had to be patient, for the following January she was still asking her husband to remember the 'thing for my neck'.

When John Paston wanted to put his male servants into new liveries his wife had to write and tell him that in the whole of Norfolk and Suffolk there was not enough of any one cloth of the colour he wanted. She also mentioned that she had not been able to find any cloth at all, either 'murrey' (which was mulberry colour, or reddish-brown), blue or russet, at less than three shillings a yard. Perhaps that does not sound very much, but it was

A fifteenth century
necklace

a great deal in the fifteenth century, as we realize when we find that a labourer's wages were only sixpence a day.

In one of her letters Margaret Paston asks her husband to buy 'some frieze to make of your children's gowns, ye should have best cheap and best choice of Haye's wife as it is told me. And that you will buy a yard of broad cloth of black for one hood for me of four shillings a yard, for there is neither good cloth nor good frieze in this town. As for the children's gowns, and I have them I will do them maken.'

Whether this means that she will make them herself or have them made by someone else is uncertain. There is no suggestion that Margaret and her daughter should spin and weave the fabric for themselves, as they would probably have done if they had lived two or three hundred years earlier.

One of John and Margaret Paston's children, another John,

133

when he was about nineteen, was an attendant on the Duke of Norfolk. In a letter to his father from Holt, Norfolk, he begs that the bearer of the letter may be given money enough to buy him (the son) a gown, for John writes: 'I have but one gown at Framlingham and another here, and that is my livery gown, and we must wear them every day for the more part, and one gown without change will soon be done.'

Sometimes, of course, the women of the family were themselves in London, and they in their turn received letters begging them to carry out commissions for those left at home. In 1465 Margaret Paston, in London, received a letter from her son John saying: 'Mother I beseech you that there may be purveyed some mean that I might have sent me home by the same messenger two pair of hose, one pair black and another pair of russet, which be ready made for me at the hosier's with the crooked back, next to the Black Friar's gate within Ludgate; John Pampynge knoweth him well enough I suppose, and the black hose be paid for he will send me the russet unpaid for; I beseech you that this gear be not forgotten, for I have not an whole hose for to don; I trow they shall cost both pair eight shillings.'

Not long after John was in such great need of hose, his sister, who lived in the household of some great lady, was in trouble because she had no neckerchiefs, and her mother had to ask her son John (who was then himself in London) to get her some as 'I can none get in this town'. Again and again this same remark appears. Even such simple things as the cords with which men tied their hose to their under-tunics, or their sleeves to the shoulders, could not be bought at Paston.

Pedlars travelled round the country with cloth and with ribbons, girdles, jewels and other ornaments. They must have been very welcome, and their arrival quite an event. Some of them carried silken fabrics, for the manufacture of silk gradually spread from Constantinople and the surrounding country to towns in Italy such as Florence, Milan, Genoa and Venice, and to such islands as Sicily. In the fifteenth century it spread to England and France. So silk fabrics were a little easier to get than they had been, though they were still expensive. No wonder some fifteenth-century men and women were tempted to buy more than they could afford, and fell into debt.

But this does not seem to have been the case with the Pastons. Their difficulty seems to have been to get any new clothes at all —particularly the women, whose menfolk needed a good deal of prodding before they remembered to buy the things they had been asked to get. The young wife of one of the John Pastons wrote to him in 1477:

'. . . my mother sent to my father in London for a gown cloth of mustyrdevyllers to make a gown for me; and he told my mother and me when he was come home, that he charged you to buy it after that he was come out of London. I pray you, if it be not bought, that you will vouchsafe to buy it and send it home as soon as ye may, for I have no gown to wear this winter but my black and my green a lyer, and that is so cumbrous that I am weary to wear it. As for the girdle that my father behested me, I spake to him thereof a little before he yed to London last, and he said to me that the fault was in you that ye would not think thereupon to do make it; I pray you, if ye dare take it upon you, that ye will vouchsafe to do make it against ye come home, for I had never more need thereof than I have now. . . .'

'To do make it' means, presumably, 'to have it made', and Margery is unwilling to believe that her husband is to blame for forgetting the girdle, but prefers to blame her father. It is uncertain what material is meant by mustyrdevyllers, but the word—in a variety of spellings—appears quite frequently in the Middle Ages. It may have been a kind of velvet, though some authorities say it was a soft, grey, woollen cloth. It is also uncertain what Margery Paston meant by 'green a lyer'.

A year later John Paston is again being begged to do some shopping, but this time by his young brother, William, a scholar at Eton: '. . . I beseech you to send me a hose cloth,' writes William, 'one for the holydays of some colour, and another for the working days how coarse soever it be maketh no matter, and a stomacher, and two shirts, and a pair of slippers; and if it like you that I may come with Alweder by water and sport me with you in London a day or two this term time, then ye may let all this be till the time that I come.'

From time to time a Paston man writes home asking that some garment—'my gown of puke furred with white lamb' or 'my long russet gown'—shall be sent to him, but naturally enough he does not describe them any more fully, much as we may wish that he had.

And the Paston women do not tell us how they intend to make up their cloth, or frieze, or mustyrdevyllers when they have at last persuaded their husbands or sons to buy it, and the carrier has brought it home over the rough tracks, probably loaded on to the back of a mule or pack-horse.

CHAPTER 14

Man Becomes Broad and Square

Most of us know what kind of clothes King Henry VIII of England wore because we have seen reproductions of a famous portrait which the painter Holbein painted of him. Henry stands solidly, looking straight out of the picture, his feet, in their flat, square-toed, almost heel-less shoes, placed well apart. He wears an outer jacket (or jerkin) made in some rich, heavy fabric, with very full skirts to the knee, and under it a short doublet (or waistcoat) which has rows of little slits all over the front of it through which his white shirt puffs out. The sleeves, also, are slashed so that the full sleeve of the shirt shows through, and between each slit is a large jewelled button or brooch. The shirt shows, too, at the neck, where it is gathered into a little band, and at the wrist.

Over everything the king wears a very full, knee-length gown, or coat, with a huge fur collar turned back at the neck and down the front. It has short but very full sleeves to the elbow. On his head he wears a flat cap with a feather across the front, and hanging down over one side. The short, wide clothes make the king look very broad and square.

Clothes like these were typical of the early sixteenth century, though less important people wore plainer materials and not so many jewels or embroideries as the king often wore.

The skirts of the jerkin were often separate, and were tied to the upper part with 'points', as the laces were called, just as the long tight hose were tied to the doublet. The sleeves, too, were often tied on at the shoulder and might be of quite a different colour and different fabric from the garment they were attached to. They were always very large and full, and besides being slashed they were 'bombasted', or stuffed, so that they were like bolsters. The sleeves of the outer robe, or coat, were very large, though they might be short or long, or open from the elbow and hanging loose. Sometimes there was no sleeve at all.

Early in the sixteenth century men's shirts and doublets were cut so low in the neck that the whole of the man's throat and

Early sixteenth century man

part of his chest were bare, but by about 1520 the shirt was gathered into the band which we see in Henry's portrait, or was finished in a little frill which, later, was to grow into the great ruff of Elizabeth's reign. Then, if the doublet was still cut low, the space between it and the neck was filled in with the stomacher, which might be embroidered or jewelled.

138

MAN BECOMES BROAD AND SQUARE

Men everywhere wore their clothes slashed so that the lining or shirt showed in little puffs. This very odd fashion is said to have started among the fighting men of Switzerland and Germany, but it spread everywhere and was popular for a very long time. At first, of course, rulers in many countries tried to stop it, but, as usual, their commands had no effect.

Even the square toes of men's shoes were stuffed and slashed. The slashings on doublets were usually arranged in neat rows, but sometimes, especially in Germany, they were arranged in patterns, such as stars and crosses. One German in 1523 described his doublet as being made of fustian and having four thousand eight hundred slits in it through which the white velvet lining showed.

The upper, or breeches, part of the long hose was stuffed and slashed and lined with silk or satin so that it formed a great roll round the hips and developed into the garments that are called trunk-hose—breeches and stockings all in one. In addition to being slashed, sleeves, doublets and the upper part of hose were often decorated with strips of velvet called 'guards'. The breeches part of the long hose varied in length and shape in different countries. It was longer in Italy than in France; wider in England than anywhere else, because more stuffed; but loose and unpadded in Germany.

Portraits which have come down to us of Henry VIII's six wives and of other ladies of the time show them in dresses cut low in the neck, generally in a square. The skirts just reached the ground all round and were made bell-shaped and rather stiff. Two or three cloth petticoats were worn under them to make them stand out, and the front of the gown was cut up the centre to show the kirtle or underskirt, which was often of magnificent material.

Women, like men, wore bombasted and slashed sleeves, with full, very wide sleeves over them, and a huge cuff, often of fur, turned back over the lower arm. The bodices were smooth and tight and were worn over a hard corset of leather or some strong material stiffened with wood or even metal.

On their heads women wore the gable head-dress, or the

French hood, which was a close-fitting cap with a stiff circlet of velvet, satin or some similar fabric standing up from it and encircling the head. A portrait of Catherine Howard, Henry VIII's fifth wife, shows her wearing a French hood. Behind each of these head-dresses hung a veil, or a velvet bag which hid the hair. Some women wore a net or cap which enclosed the hair

Early sixteenth century woman

and, over it, very much on one side, a flat feather-trimmed hat which was exactly like those worn by men, and which was sometimes small and sometimes very large indeed.

Clothes like those we have been describing were worn all over Europe, though they differed in detail from country to country. It is not always easy for us, centuries later, to tell exactly what the differences were, but they were obvious to the people of the time—just as we can often tell to-day, by the shape of his coat, the size of his hat, or some other little detail, whether a man is an American, an Englishman, a Frenchman or a German, even though their clothes may be very much alike. In early sixteenth-century descriptions of people we often read of a garment being 'in the French style', or being cut 'as worn in Germany', but with no other explanation.

Nevertheless, we know that sleeves were bigger in England than in Germany—England seems to have exaggerated every fashion that came to her from abroad—that Italian doublets were longer and had wider skirts than the German; that Italians gave up the low neck for men earlier than the Germans did, and the Germans earlier than the French. In every country we read indignant protests against the aping of 'foreign fashions'. The people of Milan are accused of copying the French, the French of copying the Italians and Spaniards, the English of copying everybody.

It was sometimes really dangerous to appear in garments that suggested one might be a foreigner, as the Reformation and the teaching of Luther had roused such strong feelings everywhere. The Protestants hated the Catholics and the Catholics hated the Protestants. A traveller describes how he was called a 'German and a Lutheran' in Venice in 1546 because of the clothes he was wearing. He hurriedly bought a fresh outfit, but on leaving Italy he and his companions narrowly escaped being murdered because of their Italian clothes, and he tells us they had to have them remade 'in the German manner' in Innsbruck.

But although there were these differences, the more cultured, travelled and educated people of all countries tended to wear clothes that, in essentials, were alike. For one thing, books about fashion began to appear in Italy, Germany, the Netherlands and France, produced by the new art of printing and illustrated with wood-cut pictures.

Nearly everyone who could afford it, even those who were not of the nobility, took a tremendous interest in clothes and spent a great deal of money on them. At Augsburg a father and son named Schwarz had their portraits painted in every new garment they bought. There are a hundred and forty of these portraits. The younger Schwarz once wrote: 'For my part, garments cannot be too out landish in shape, for the more extraordinary the cut of hose, doublet and shoe, the more I like wearing them.' A great many people seem to have felt like that.

The wealthy and noble competed with each other in the luxury of their clothes. When Henry VIII of England and Francis I of France arranged a meeting, the whole affair was so extravagant and luxurious that it has ever since been called the 'Field of the Cloth of Gold'. We are told that the two kings changed their clothes twice every day, and neither of them wore any fabric but cloth of gold or silver damask.

There is a description in existence of Francis I's return to Paris after the meeting, dressed in cloth of silver, with his nobles and marshals clothed in similar materials, his knights in crimson or black velvet embroidered in gold, and his archers in white cloth or satin embroidered with silver lilies.

When Henry VIII's sister married Louis XII of France the whole court wore gold brocade, and when Francis I's niece Jeanne, who was only thirteen years old, married the Duke of Cleves she wore a cloth-of-gold dress embroidered with silver flowers which, with her jewellery, was so heavy that she could not walk and had to be carried into the church. We read of another noble lady whose dress was so stiff with pearls that when she attended a wedding she was unable to kneel down.

Sometimes it is difficult to believe the statements which have come down to us about the quantities of precious stones and of gold and silver fabrics worn at this time. But they are confirmed by contemporary pictures and the wills, accounts and inventories of the time. One lady's stomacher, for instance, was embroidered with forty-four pearls, fourteen diamonds and fourteen rubies. Henry VIII, when he went to meet the unfortunate lady who had come to England to be his fourth wife, Anne of Cleves, wore a velvet coat so smothered with gold embroidery that the fabric itself was no longer visible, and his buttons were of diamonds, rubies and pearls. All the king's shirts were embroidered at the neck with gold.

Francis I ordered thirteen thousand six hundred small gold buttons to trim a black velvet outfit, and another French king had eighteen dozen large silver buttons made for him in the form of skulls. Buttons were often studded with diamonds or other precious stones, and the laces, or 'points' which were used to attach sleeves to garments, hose to doublets and so on were given golden tags which were also set with pearls and other

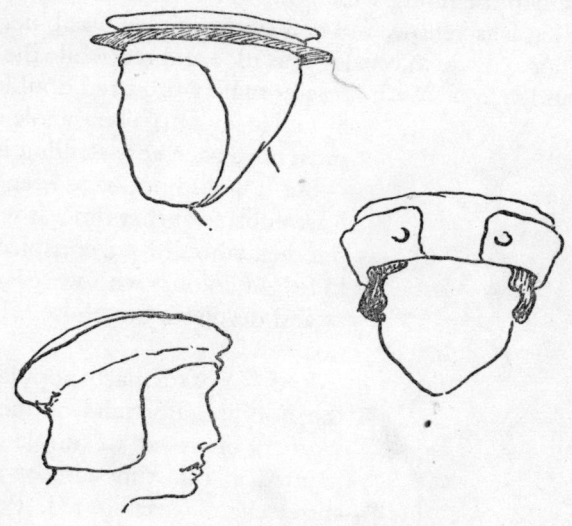

Tudor hats

gems. Pearls were especially valued and enormous quantities were used. There were all kinds of superstitions about them, and they and other gems were even supposed to be capable of healing the sick. Pope Clement VII, who died in 1534, swallowed crushed pearls and gems worth enormous sums during the two weeks before his death.

Of course, less wealthy people could not smother themselves with precious stones as kings and queens did. But they wore the richest fabrics and furs they could afford, used a great deal of embroidery, and slashed, puffed and bombasted their clothes as much as they possibly could, especially the sleeves.

In the early part of the century, when a great deal of the shirt was visible, women often embroidered the fronts and collars of shirts which they presented as gifts to their men friends and relations. The elder Schwarz bought himself, in 1520, a shirt with sleeves a yard wide, of which the whole of the front and collar were embroidered in gold. Men wore extraordinary mixtures of colours. In 1521 Schwarz bought himself a pair of green hose of which the lining which puffed through the slashings on the right leg was yellow, and that of the left leg was blue. Later he wore hose of which one leg was blue and red while the other was red and yellow. With these hose he wore a red doublet and

a violet cloak. The whole effect must have been very striking indeed —but it would not have been in the least unusual at that time. It was not the men who dressed conspicuously in bright colours who were laughed at and despised, but those who did not.

Red was particularly popular with the nobility. Portraits of men and women of royal or noble blood painted at this time almost always show them wearing red. Peasants were not allowed to wear it. One of the demands made by the European peasants who revolted against the nobility in the early part of the sixteenth century was that this ban should be removed.

The full gown, or overcoat, often with a fur collar or lining, which Henry VIII wears in his portrait, was very popular indeed, not only among the nobility but among the

Long gown worn by men in the sixteenth century

middle classes. Students, teachers and preachers, including Luther, wore it, but of ankle length. Holbein, in a portrait he painted of himself as a young man, is wearing it—though without a fur collar—and in his portrait of Erasmus the great scholar is shown wearing two such gowns one on top of another. Holbein's fine picture in the National Gallery, London, called 'The Ambassadors' shows this garment in its two forms, one knee length and one reaching the ground.

Thick, heavy gold chains were often worn round the neck in the first half of the sixteenth century. Sometimes brides and bridegrooms presented them to one another at the wedding ceremony. Occasionally, among the rich and great, a very rare and valuable possession hung on the chain—a watch. Watches had only recently been invented, at Nuremberg in Germany. King Henry VIII wore one, and it is said that the Emperor Charles V wore a small striking watch attached to an ear-ring. But watches were few and far between. It is rather surprising to read of a man having attached to his knee, not a watch, but an hour glass, while another had a quarter-hour glass in the handle of a riding-whip.

Some of the simpler styles worn in England in early Tudor times by ordinary people have survived to this day almost as they were in the early sixteenth century. In the Tower of London we can see 'Beefeaters', or Yeomen of the Guard, to give them their real title, wearing red, full-skirted tunics and flat hats almost exactly like those worn by their forerunners, the personal bodyguards of the first Tudor kings. But on their breasts the rose, thistle and shamrock are embroidered now, whilst the Tudor yeomen had only the combined red and white roses of York and Lancaster, to symbolize the end of the Wars of the

A Beefeater

Roses. The ruff round the neck was added in Elizabeth's time.

Others who wear clothes very like those of the sixteenth century are the boys who are pupils at Christ's Hospital—the 'blue-coat boys' as they are called. They wear long gowns of blue cloth, buttoned to the waist, with a stand-up collar and a leather belt. Under the gown, nowadays, they wear knee-breeches and yellow stockings, but the first pupils would have worn a close-fitting doublet and hose tied to it at the waist with laces. Until the nineteenth century they wore the flat woollen cap with a narrow brim which was the usual headgear for men and boys in the sixteenth century.

blue-coat boy of Tudor times

CHAPTER 15

Bombast, Farthingales and Ruffs

During the first quarter of the sixteenth century the broad full fashions we have been reading about (which originated in Germany) were worn nearly everywhere, but after that time the influence of Spain began to make itself felt.

Spain was becoming the wealthiest and most powerful country in Europe, and from 1519 her king not only ruled Spain but also Germany, the Netherlands, parts of Italy, and the new world which Columbus had discovered on the other side of the Atlantic. So it is not surprising that Spanish ideas about clothes began to spread.

Not that the great lord of all these domains, the Emperor Charles V, made any attempt to encourage the wearing of Spanish fashions. Whilst most noblemen were competing with one another in the brilliance and extravagance of their clothes, Charles amazed people by the plainness and even shabbiness of his. He wore simple, serviceable fustian without embroidery or jewellery, and it was rumoured, with horror, that he even had his clothes mended!

The Venetian ambassador reported that the great emperor could hardly have been worse dressed, that his clothes were black, of poor cloth, that there was not a shred of silk on him anywhere, and that his hat was of plain felt.

No wonder that a man who brought a horse to Charles V as a gift presented it by mistake to a finely dressed courtier instead of to the plainly dressed emperor!

When Charles V did find it necessary to dress a little better, he took very great care of his clothes. Once when he was reviewing troops he wore a velvet hat and a black cloak trimmed with velvet. But it began to rain, so the emperor whipped off his hat and put it under his cloak and sat with the rain beating down on his head until a plain grey cloak and grey felt hat had been brought to him.

The Spanish-type doublet which gradually became fashionable was narrower and more close-fitting than those worn by King Henry VIII and his contemporaries, and was without the full skirts. Sleeves, too, were tighter, with rolls, or wings, at the shoulders which were often cut into little sections, or tabs. Doublets were still slashed, but the linings were flatter and were not puffed out through the slashings. The jerkin fitted closely over the doublet and was often sleeveless, or had hanging, or sometimes mock, sleeves. Both jerkins and doublets were usually buttoned, laced or hooked up the front, but some opened at the sides.

Late sixteenth century

Men often wore a short circular cloak. Sometimes the cloak was like a mock coat, as it had sleeves which simply hung down the back when the garment was thrown round the shoulders.

Fashionable men wore hats with tall crowns and narrow brims in place of the flat hats of a little earlier, but humbler men went on wearing the flat woollen caps, and English apprentices were compelled by law to wear them.

The upper-stocks (which was what the breeches section of the trunk-hose was called) were, at first, quite short and were padded or stuffed to make them the shape of pumpkins or melons. The long stocking was still attached to the breeches,

BOMBAST, FARTHINGALES AND RUFFS

but gradually men began to wear breeches, which they called hose, and stockings, which they called nether-stocks, as separate garments. The hose were then a variety of shapes and lengths, from the very short melon-shaped trunk-hose to 'Venetians', which were knee-breeches fastened below the knee, with the stocking drawn up over them and rolled over the garter which held them firmly. Sometimes Venetians were smooth and pad-

An Elizabethan short cloak

ded to a kind of pear shape; sometimes they were fuller and looser and unpadded.

Trunk-hose were often 'paned', which means that the material was cut into strips which showed the lining, under which came the padding. By the middle of the century soldiers in the camp of the Elector of Saxony at Magdeburg were wearing knee-breeches which consisted of strips of cloth unjoined from waist to knee, and lined with very full breeches of a light material, usually silk.

Men's hats in Elizabeth I's time

149

We can still see clothes of this strange sixteenth-century style in Rome to-day, for they are worn by the Pope's bodyguard. The members of the Swiss Guard, as they are called, stand on duty outside the Vatican, and their uniform consists of doublets and hose made up of alternate strips of blue and yellow cloth over a bright red lining—though the lining does not hang out as loosely as was often the case in the sixteenth century, when it sometimes drooped down between the cloth strips al-

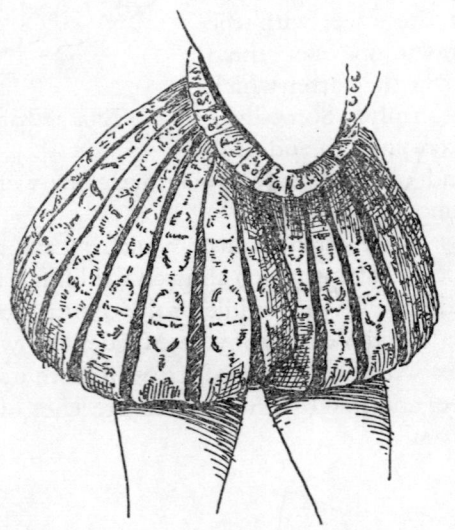

Sixteenth century trunk hose

most to the ankles. Often the linings of the two legs were of different colours.

Some rulers tried to discredit these 'plunderhose' as they were called, by dressing their hangmen in them; others imprisoned the men who wore them. But nothing had any effect, and plunderhose continued in fashion for about thirty years. The exaggeratedly floppy ones do not appear to have been worn much outside Germany.

Sometimes short trunk-hose, when they did not have long

nether-stocks attached to them, had two tube-like pieces of cloth instead which covered the wearer's thighs. The stockings were then drawn up over them and gartered.

The Spanish court at this time was rather a grim and serious place, so quiet, sober colours were worn. But although the shapes of Spanish clothes were copied in other countries, in many

Plunderhose   One of the Pope's bodyguard

places outside Spain people went on wearing bright colours, and, if they were wealthy, a good deal of cloth-of-gold and silver. In France light colours, including white, were worn, sometimes a dozen shades in one outfit, and costumes were changed so often that a courtier must possess at least twenty-five complete outfits. In England bright colours were popular, and certain districts became famous for certain dyes—Bristol for red, for instance, and Kendal for green. Coventry was known for its blue cloth, which was worn by serving-men and apprentices.

Spanish fashions spread over Europe in spite of the fact that so many people were resisting Spain, either because they had become Protestants and Catholic Spain was trying to force them back to the old faith, or because her armies and navies prevented them from trading freely in the New World.

A sixteenth century lady wearing a Spanish farthingale

In England Queen Mary married Philip II of Spain in 1553, and although many Englishmen disapproved of the marriage it did not stop them from wearing Spanish fashions—and exaggerating them. Trunk-hose were worn larger in England than anywhere else. They were stuffed under the silk lining with horse-hair, rags, or anything that came handy, including bran. There is a story told of a man who sat on a chair from which a nail protruded. When his sovereign entered and he rose to his feet the nail tore a large hole in his breeches and the bran poured out in a stream round his feet, much to his embarrassment.

Women's dresses became wider, too, and from Mary's reign the 'Spanish farthingale' was worn under the skirt to hold it out. At first the farthingale was probably a strong petticoat stiffened with hoops of cane, but later it became a framework of iron or steel. The outer skirt was still split in front in order to show

Head-dresses worn by Elizabethan women

the kirtle. Both women's gowns and men's doublets, during the second half of the century, were usually worn high at the neck.

But the most striking feature of the period was the ruff which was worn almost everywhere by both men and women from the 1550s onwards. It started as a mere frill at the neck of the shirt or chemise, then it became a separate article of clothing, small at first but gradually becoming larger and larger among fashionable people as time went on. Spoons had to be made with extra long handles so that people in cart-wheel ruffs could feed themselves easily.

Ruffs were not easy to make—or to wear. A shower of rain might reduce them to bits of rag flapping round the wearer's shoulders. At first the only way of stiffening them was with fine wire, and they were also supported by an 'under-propper', a framework of wire covered with fabric.

When Queen Elizabeth heard of a Flemish woman who was especially clever at making ruffs, and who, moreover, knew the

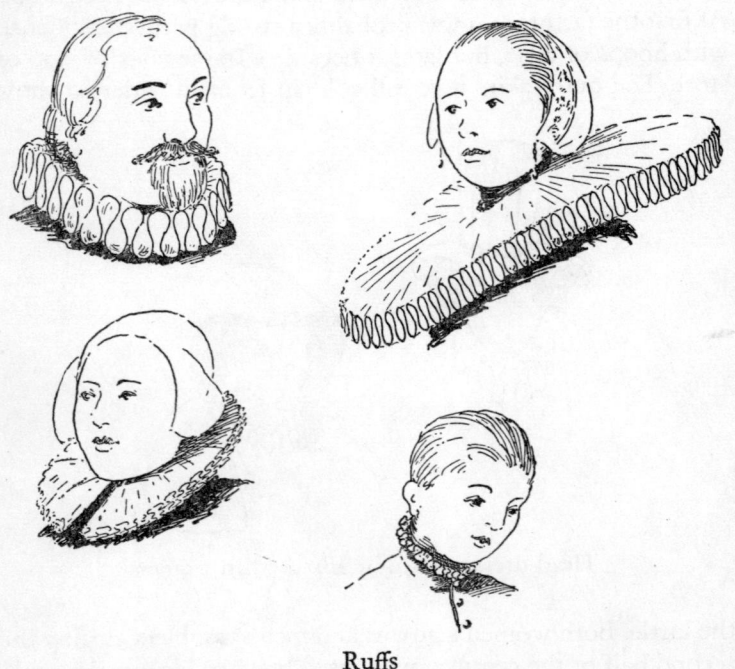

Ruffs

secret of how to keep them stiff without wire, she sent for her. The secret was starching, which was unknown until that time. The Flemish woman gave lessons in ruff-making to English ladies at £4 to £5 a lesson, and charged them another £1 for teaching them the art of starching. At first the starch was of a bluish colour. An Englishwoman named Mistress Turner invented a method of making the starch yellow, or saffron colour.

Saffron ruffs became very fashionable. It is said that in France bluish starched ruffs were worn by Catholics and saffron ones by Protestants, or Huguenots as they were called. But Mistress Turner was tried and found guilty of murder, and was hanged wearing a saffron ruff. After that saffron coloured ruffs went out of favour in England.

Of course, many preachers and writers disapproved of the ruff. A man named Philip Stubbs wrote a book called *The Anatomie of Abuses* in which he criticized most of the habits of his fellow men and women. This is what he had to say about ruffs:

'They have great and monstrous ruffs, made either of cambric, holland, lawne or else of so other the finest cloth that can be got with money, whereof some be a quarter of a yard deep, yea, some more, very few less, so that they stand a full quarter of a yard (and more) from their necks, hanging over their shoulder points instead of a veile. But if Aeolus with his blasts or with his storms, chance to hit upon the crazy barque of their brused ruffs, they then go flip flap in the wind like ragges that fly abroad, lying on their shoulders like the dishcloute of a slut. But wot you what? The Devil, as he in the fulness of his malice, first invented these great ruffs, so hath he now found out also two great pillars to bear up and maintain this his kingdom of pride withal (for the Devil is king and prince over all the children of pride). The one arch or pillar whereby his kingdom of great ruffs is under-propped is a certain kind of liquid matter, which they call starch, whereby the Devil hath willed them to wash and dive their ruffs well, which, being dry, will then stand stiff and inflexible round their necks. The other pillar is a certain divice made of wires, whipped over either with gold, thread, silver or silk, and this he calleth a supportasse or underpropper. This is to be applied round about their necks under the ruff, upon the outside of the band, to bear up the whole frame and body of the ruff, from falling and hanging down.'

One thing that encouraged the development of the ruff was the fact that about this time people learnt how to make something quite new for the adornment of their clothes. It was lace.

A support for a ruff

For years open-work patterns had been worked in linen, and the warp threads projecting from a piece of material after it had been cut from the loom had been knotted and plaited in fringes of various kinds. But the making of true bobbin and needle-point lace dates only from the sixteenth century. No one knows for certain where it started, but it was possibly in Italy.

Lace became very popular indeed. It was used to trim all kinds of things from shirts, collars and caps to sheets and tablecloths. Ladies who had previously spent much of their time doing embroidery now learnt to make lace also, and many women found in lace-making a way of earning money at home. In fact, in the Netherlands, Philip II tried to stop women making lace because he was afraid they would soon refuse to become domestic servants. But in spite of Philip II's prohibition the Netherlands became famous for its lace because it was there that the best flax was grown and the finest, whitest linen thread was produced. The popularity of the ruff all over Europe caused an enormous demand for lace, and not only poor women in their homes made it, but nuns in their convents.

Huge ruffs made of lace, or edged with lace, were very expensive indeed, and one French courtier said once that he was 'wearing thirty-two acres of the best vineyard soil' about his neck, meaning that his lace ruff cost as much as a thirty-two-acre estate would have done.

But it was not only the fine and dainty lace used on ruffs that was popular, but rich gold lace to trim the gowns and coats of heavy damask and brocade. King Henry III of France is said to have had four thousand yards of real gold lace on his person on one occasion—though this seems difficult to believe.

BOMBAST, FARTHINGALES AND RUFFS

Queen Elizabeth I of England loved lace and possessed an enormous quantity of it, as she did of all other articles of adornment. Her subjects gave her presents of costly foreign lace and very soon after she became queen in 1558 we hear of her being presented with a ruff trimmed with lace and set with rubies and pearls.

Nevertheless she followed the example of other kings and queens in trying to tell her subjects how they should dress, and passed laws forbidding them to wear lace. She also forbade the wearing of very large ruffs, although her own were the largest in Europe—except, perhaps, for those worn by Margaret of Valois, Queen of Navarre. She loved clothes and finery just as much as Elizabeth did, and although she followed the fashions of her time, she also led them. For instance, she would not wear the high-necked bodice which was worn in Spain and elsewhere, but preferred to wear a low, square-cut neck, and to divide the ruff in front so that it outlined the opening. She was imitated, of course, and Elizabeth of England is shown wearing the low-cut bodice in her later portraits, with a high, stiff, upstanding ruff behind her head.

Because people used lace, it does not mean that they stopped using embroidery. In England they were particularly fond of working trailing stems and flowers in black on linen for hoods, shirts, bodices and so on, and this Elizabethan black work became quite famous. You can see some of it in the Victoria and Albert Museum in London—also some similar designs worked in colours.

In the 1570s a new kind of farthingale was worn, first in France. It was in the form of a hoop several feet across, flattened back and front, tied round the wearer's waist, and tilted downwards slightly towards the front. The tremendously wide skirt was held out from the wearer's body by the hoop, and then hung straight down to the ground, so that the effect was barrel-shaped. Some women tied a kind of bolster round their hips under their dresses instead of wearing the farthingale.

With this 'French farthingale' women wore a stiff stomacher that came to a point several inches below the waist. Men's doublets came to a point in front too, but they were also stuffed and pouched so that they formed a kind of hook which stood out several inches from the wearer's body and hung down over his belt. This extraordinary garment was called a 'peascod' doublet. You can see what it was like if you look at pictures of Punch, or you can see a real peascod doublet in the London

The French farthingale

Museum in Kensington Palace in London. The short doublets of this time generally had little short skirts which were often divided into a number of separate tabs, or 'tassets'.

Queen Elizabeth possessed a great many very elaborate gowns lavishly trimmed with pearls and other gems. She left some three thousand dresses at her death—but it is only fair to remember that many of them were presented to her by wealthy lords in whose houses she stayed or by the boroughs or towns she visited, which vied with each other in the costliness and gorgeousness of their gifts. Nowadays we feel that a lavish display of jewels, colours and costly fabrics is ostentatious, but that was not the point of view of men and women of Tudor and Elizabethan times.

Men wore their hair short, out of the way of the ruff, and

Clothes worn by Sir Walter Raleigh and his son

women finally gave up wearing head-dresses with veils hanging down the back. They took to puffing their hair out at the sides, often frizzing it, and dressing it high on their heads, often over wire frames. Sometimes they decorated it with jewels and other ornaments, and quite often they dyed it red or saffron, or wore false hair or wigs. They did not worry about making the dyed hair or the wigs look natural—in fact they would wear different coloured wigs on different days, just as they felt inclined. Elizabeth herself is said to have possessed eighty wigs.

On their heads women wore flat head-dresses, rather bonnet-shaped, or hats similar to those worn by men, or else they went about bare-headed. A Dutchman who visited England in 1575 wrote:

'The women are beautiful, fair, well-dressed and modest, which is seen there more than elsewhere, as they go about the streets without any covering either of huke or mantle, head veil or the like. Married women only wear a hat both in the street and in the house; those unmarried go without a hat, although ladies of distinction have lately learned to cover their faces with silken masks, or vizards.'

The masks he mentions were often of black velvet. They had a button inside which the wearer held in her mouth to keep the mask in place. Women of the sixteenth century carried fans. They were rectangular and attached to a long handle, so that they looked rather like stiff little flags.

From Spain, in the sixteenth century, came the first knitted silk stockings. They were very costly for a long time, and only the very richest could possess them. A Mistress Montague presented a pair of black knitted silk stockings to Queen Elizabeth fairly early in her reign, and she was so delighted with them that she would never wear any other kind afterwards. A few years earlier Sir Thomas Gresham had presented a pair of long knitted silk hose to her brother, King Edward VI.

Most people had to be content to wear woollen stockings, which were knitted by hand. Knitting probably started in Arabia, and it had been practised at least since the second century A.D. Fragments of knitted fabric dating from about that time have been found, and knitted socks, with turned heels, dating from a few centuries later. By the Middle Ages knitting, in Europe, was an important trade, carried on by men who formed themselves into guilds just as shoemakers, tailors and other craftsmen did. They had to serve for three years as apprentices and three years as journeymen (employed men, working under a master), after which they had thirteen weeks in which to do their masterpieces, or test pieces, to see if they were fit to be masters. For this they had to make a carpet about five yards square, patterned with flowers or something similar; a beret or cap; a woollen shirt and a pair of hose decorated with clocks up the sides.

Towards the end of the sixteenth century a clergyman named William Lee invented a stocking frame or machine by means of which knitting could be done much more quickly. He started a stocking knitting business at Bunhill Fields in London, and Queen Elizabeth went to see it. But the stockings knitted by Lee's machine were not so fine as those knitted by hand, and the queen did not like them. Lord Hunsden begged the queen to grant Lee a patent for the making of stockings, but she refused, as so many people earned their living by knitting stockings by hand.

At that time no encouragement at all was given to ingenious people such as Lee. In Danzig a man invented a little machine for making ribbon, but the rulers of the city had him drowned in the river because they thought his invention would do harm to the craftsmen who made ribbon by hand. Lee was not treated quite so badly, but as he could not use his stocking frames in England he went to France, where he died some time later.

However, one valuable little machine that had been invented and used on the continent since about the 1470s did find its way to England during the sixteenth century. It was the spinning-wheel. In time the distaff and spindle, which women had used ever since the New Stone Age, were forgotten, and the whir of the spinning-wheel was heard wherever thread was produced.

By this time English ships were carrying English cloth to ports in the Mediterranean, and the English 'Merchant Adventurers', as they were called, were sending their ships northward to ports in Russia, southward to the coasts of Africa, and westward to the New World, to find new places in which to trade. Some of the cloth merchants became very wealthy indeed.

Another innovation of the sixteenth century was that, to us, commonplace necessity the handkerchief. Handkerchiefs, like forks and other refined things, are said to have originated in Italy. Then they travelled to Germany and over the rest of Europe. But they, too, were at first costly and rare luxuries. In one sixteenth-century will, an Englishman gives careful instructions for the disposal of his *two* Dutch handkerchiefs.

Shoes of the latter part of the sixteenth century were generally fairly round at the toe, and were higher than those worn earlier, covering the instep up to the ankles. At first they were slashed. After about 1575 shoes became a little nearer to the kind of shoe we wear now, with two side-pieces of leather joined on the instep with laces, with a small tongue in between.

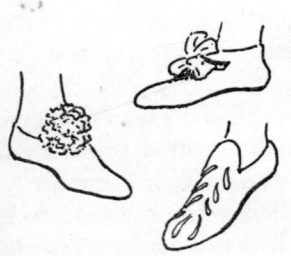

Elizabethan shoes   A chopine

Pantoffles, which were like slippers into which the front part of the foot could be slipped, had cork soles which were thicker at the heel than at the toe, and they were worn to protect the finer and more delicate shoes, especially, of course, out of doors.

About 1600 heels such as we know began to be attached to shoes and boots, at first for riding but later for ordinary everyday wear.

Chopines, which originated in Italy, probably Venice, were shoes on wooden stands three to four inches high, which were gaily painted with flowers and other patterns in bright colours. Chopines were very difficult to walk in, and we read that

Venetian ladies had to be supported on each side by a servant when they went out.

Gloves were worn more than before. Some were of silk, but leather gloves with a gauntlet were more popular. The Bodleian Library in Oxford has a pair of gloves of white leather stitched with gold that belonged to Queen Elizabeth. A pair which belonged to Mary, Queen of Scots, are embroidered with silver and coloured silks. The finest gloves came from Spain and were very highly prized. They were often given as presents to the great and powerful, or were left to people in wills. They were very often perfumed.

In 1577 Lady Grey gave Queen Elizabeth two pairs of Spanish gloves decorated with four dozen gold buttons, each set with a real pearl, and the following year the queen received another pair on which were two dozen gold buttons each of which had a diamond inset.

By the end of the sixteenth century the authorities everywhere were becoming more worried than ever at the disappearance of class distinctions in dress. Nearly all rulers, teachers and preachers, Catholic, Protestant, Puritan or whatever they might be, considered it vitally important that each class in the community should be clearly recognizable at sight. So towns and provinces in almost every country made regulations laying down in the minutest detail what materials and trimmings each class might wear and what shapes, styles and even colours their clothes and hats should be.

In England, under Elizabeth, men with less than £40 a year were forbidden to bombast their doublets and were ordered to wear flat woollen caps on their heads. But it was still very difficult to enforce these regulations except in a few cases. All the same, most ordinary working people did not attempt to wear the exaggeratedly puffed, slashed and padded garments worn by the nobility, and they certainly could not deck themselves out with expensive jewels and feathers.

Collars, or bands as they were called, were worn at the neck in place of the ruff by servants and working people. Professional and middle-class people often wore ruffs which were small and neat. Students, statesmen, merchants and such-like sober men still wore long gowns with long, open sleeves, similar to those of earlier times, though the wings or rolls on the shoulders and the small ruffs at the neck would show that they were living in the last half of the sixteenth century. Servants, pensioners, schoolboys and people of that kind wore the long, full-skirted blue coat which the boys of Christ's Hospital still wear. Usually such people wore collars instead of ruffs.

Countrywomen, such as farmers' wives, had far too much to do to worry very much about fashions. Books of instruction and advice to sixteenth-century housewives that have come down to us make us wonder whether she ever had any leisure at all, and whether it was really possible for any woman to possess all the virtues considered necessary. One such book tells us that an English housewife must be 'of chaste thought, stout courage, patient, untired, watchful, diligent, witty, pleasant, constant in friendship, full of good neighbourhood, wise in discourse, but not frequent therein, sharp and quick of speech, but not bitter or talkative, secret in her affairs, confortable in her counsels, and generally skilful in all the worthy knowledges which do belong to her vocation'.

It is not surprising, after all that, that the writer tells her that her garments should be 'comely, cleanly and strong, made as well to preserve the health as adorn the person, altogether without toyish garnishes or the gloss of light colours, and as far from the vanity of new and fantastic fashions, as near to the comely imitations of modest matrons'.

Another book of the time which describes people in many walks of life, and the way in which they lived, speaks of the shepherd and says: 'His flock affords him his whole raiment, outside and linings, cloth and leather; and instead of much costly linen, his little garden yields hemp enough to make his lockram shirts.'

CHAPTER 16

Cavalier Elegance and Puritan Plainness

For the first quarter of the seventeenth century clothes did not change very much. Men still wore tight, stiff, bombasted doublets with a point in front and a little narrow, or tabbed, skirt, flaring out over the hips—though the actual peascod doublet gradually lost favour. Hose were very full and baggy, and were still stuffed out to an enormous size. The short melon-shaped trunk-hose died out (except that they were sometimes worn by pages and young serving-men) and hose were usually knee-length. They were laced on to the doublet at the waist, the laces forming a series of bows on the outside of the doublet. Women went on wearing farthingales and tight, pointed bodices just as they had done towards the end of the sixteenth century. Ruffs, not quite so large as before, were worn by both sexes.

Men escaped before women did from the Spanish fashions which had been worn since the middle of the sixteenth century, and which continued to be worn in Spain and in the parts of Europe ruled by, or under the influence of, Spain.

But Spain no longer had the power or influence she had had a century earlier. In the Netherlands, for instance, men had won their freedom from Spanish domination. The Dutch, who had become Protestants, had been persecuted by the Catholic Spaniards, so they wanted nothing that would remind them of Spain. Holland became both powerful and wealthy, and for a time the simpler clothes worn by well-to-do Dutch citizens and their wives were imitated in most other countries.

Men's clothes became looser and softer, and with the waist in the natural place. The skirt of the doublet became longer and often consisted of a number of tabs that widened out from the waist and overlapped. Round about 1620 the ruff was deprived of its starch and its wire supports and became a 'falling ruff' which hung down in pleats from just below the chin on to the shoulders. Many men took to wearing a "standing band"—a

A standing band

An early seventeenth century boy

A falling ruff

large, flat, stiffened collar, high up round the neck, which made the head look as though it were resting on a dish or plate. In Spain this flat collar was called a 'golilla', and after 1623, when the Spanish Government forbade the wearing of lace, it was the collar usually worn. The fine portraits which the great Spanish artist Velasquez painted of Philip IV of Spain nearly all show the king wearing a golilla.

Over their doublets men wore jerkins, or jackets, that were usually sleeveless. Those worn for riding, fighting and so on were often made of leather and were called 'buff jerkins'. Round their waists men wore wide sashes, even over leather jerkins, and over their shoulders they had a sword-belt, either of leather or of embroidered silk.

Just below their knees they wore wide ribbon garters with big bows at the side, and on their shoes there were rosettes which gradually became larger and larger. The toes of the shoes became square, and both men and women wore high heels, which were often painted red.

Early seventeenth century shoe

Wooden clogs, or pattens, were made with a well at the back to receive the high heel of the shoe. Such pattens were worn by most people in bad weather to protect the leather or cloth shoes, and they naturally made a great clatter in paved streets or on stone floors. Until as late as last century notices could be seen in church porches, 'Ladies are required to take off their pattens before entering.'

Many country people wore wooden clogs without any other shoe, and stuffed them with straw. Such clogs can still be seen in some places, such as Holland and Brittany.

But boots were very popular, too. At first they were often very long, and although they fitted the leg fairly well as far as the knee, above that they were so wide that they fell back to show the lining, and must have been very difficult to walk in. Later they were shortened to about the middle of the calf, but still widened out into a kind of funnel.

Boot and shoe making became an even more highly skilled craft than it had been before—and boot repairing, too. Cobblers, like pedlars, travelled from place to place, carrying their tools in a basket, and when they found a job to do they sat down very often on the doorstep and sang while they worked, or told the latest news to the people of the house, who we can be sure listened with eager interest.

Seventeenth century boots

Inside their boots men wore 'boot-hose' or socks, over their other stockings, and these boot-hose were often elaborately trimmed at the top with embroidery and flounces of lace. The boots themselves, even, were often given coloured, embroidered or lace-edged linings which cost enormous sums. Shoe rosettes also cost a great deal. An English writer of 1638 mentions a pair costing £30.

Sleeves were generally full at the shoulder and laced to the garment, as they had been before, and they tapered to the wrist, where they were finished with a wide white cuff. At first the upper part of the sleeve had several long slashes all round as far as the elbow, but later men's sleeves usually had one long slash all the way down from shoulder to wrist, with buttons and loops on either side which could be fastened if the wearer liked. The outer side of the legs of breeches was treated in the same way.

Sometimes, after the 1630s, men wore narrow straight trousers which hung loose to a few inches below the knee, where they were finished with bows or frills. After about that time, too, the breeches were attached to the inside of the doublets by means of hooks and eyes, so that the bows round the waists of doublets were nothing but ornament. Some doublets were almost straight and rather short, and were buttoned up only for

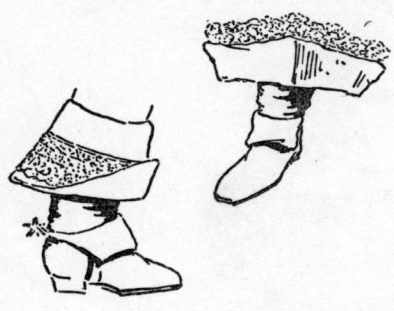

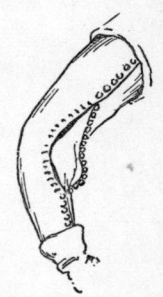

Boots and hose trimmed with lace   A buttoned sleeve

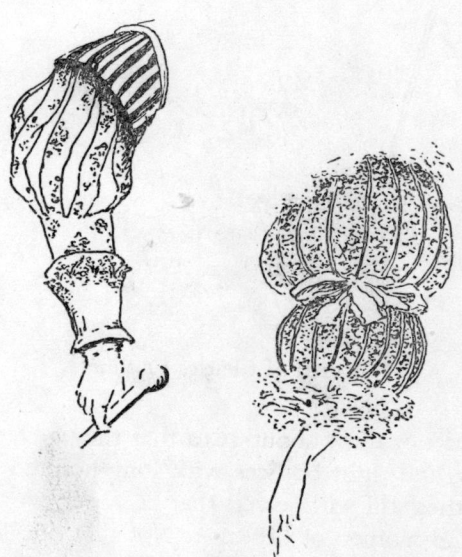

A man's and a woman's sleeve of the seventeenth century

a few inches at the top, after which they opened to reveal a triangle of shirt above the breeches.

Women went on wearing ruffs after men had given them up, but they also wore the standing band and the falling ruff, as men did, often with gowns cut low at the neck. They also went on wearing the upstanding fan-shaped ruff, outlining the neck of the

A man of Charles I's time

dress. It was not until about 1630 that they gave up wearing farthingales, and tight bodices with long-pointed stomachers, and the clothes stiff with jewels that had been worn by Queen Elizabeth and women of her time. Not that one must believe that the precious stones shown in portraits were always quite so lavishly distributed on the original dresses. We are told that some English ladies paid their portrait painter ten shillings extra to paint a fine string of pearls round their necks, and a lady of the time wrote to a friend that, in his portrait of her, Van Dyck had given her far more diamonds than she possessed.

But by the end of the 1620s women everywhere except in Spain had begun to discard the farthingale and the padded rolls which some of them had worn round their waists instead of farthingales. Then their skirts fell in folds from their waists without any stiffening to make them stand out, though, of course, they wore several petticoats under them. Their bodices often had little skirts or basques as we now call them, similar to the men's. They continued to wear pointed stomachers, often with the bodice of the upper gown laced over them.

Woman of Charles I's time

The high neck of the Spanish dress was finally given up almost everywhere, and dresses were cut low. But at first a wide, plain, transparent collar which fitted close to the neck was often worn over the low-necked dress. This was one of the fashions which originated in Holland, and many Dutch portraits show women dressed in this way.

Another Dutch fashion that was adopted in other countries in the first half of the seventeenth century was that of wearing black instead of the wide variety of bright colours all combined in one outfit which had been considered elegant. Many portraits of the time show men and women wearing black. They also show women wearing, indoors, short velvet 'house coats' trimmed with fur, which also became very popular in Holland.

But one of the most surprising changes in women's dress at this time was that for the first time for hundreds of years women began to show their wrists and a few inches of their arms. Even before they gave up the farthingale they began to wear sleeves slightly shorter than they had ever been before since early Christian times. At first the sleeves were still large and stiff, like bolsters, though they were sometimes tied in the middle to form two puffs. But the puffing and the ribbons disappeared by about 1630, and a fairly full, loose, three-quarter-length sleeve, finished with a white cuff or lace frill, was usually worn.

The shorter sleeves led to the introduction of long, soft gloves for women, and even with long sleeves women began to wear soft gloves without a stiff gauntlet. Men still wore gauntleted gloves—in fact they seem to have had a passion for them, and members of the nobility had vast numbers. The eldest son of James I of England, Prince Henry, who died young, is said to have used thirty-one pairs of perfumed, decorated gloves in one year when he was only fourteen. He also had, in one year, thirty-eight suits of velvet, silk and satin, which cost about two thousand pounds, and thirteen mantles costing about fifty pounds each.

So much money was squandered on clothes that we hear of certain families in Germany uniting together and vowing that none of them would wear any garment costing more than a certain sum which they all decided was reasonable.

After 1625 all clothes became less stiff and tight. Bombasting was given up altogether, and gradually the ruff almost disappeared, though elderly and staid men, certain officials and clergymen, continued to wear it for a long time, and some women were still wearing it in the 1660s. In fact, in England, the choristers of Salisbury Cathedral, and the Yeomen of the Guard, still wear it.

But after about 1630 most women, and men too, took to wearing very wide collars, or 'bands' as they called them, which might be of expensive lace if the wearer was wealthy, or plain linen if he was not. Such collars were worn with doublets and jerkins, over cloaks and long gowns, and even over armour.

Outdoors men and women wore long, wide cloaks, which sometimes had wide collars.

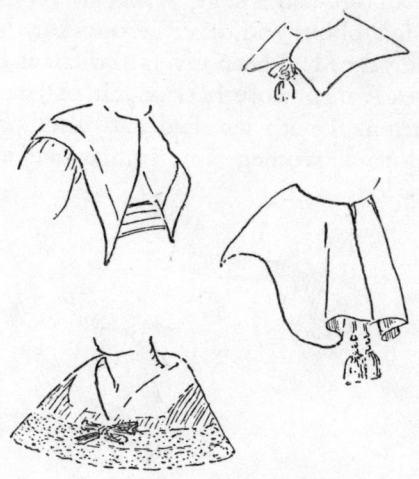

Seventeenth century collars

At first women's skirts were still divided up the centre to show the under-dress, but later they were usually joined up. Then it became fashionable to have them very long, so that for walking or any kind of work they had to be bunched up and held by the wearer, or thrown over her arm, or tucked into her belt, thus showing the elaborate petticoat worn under them. Then some women began to open up the front of the skirt again, and to pouch the two sides up out of the way when necessary.

While people wore ruffs the men cut their hair short and women wore theirs dressed high on their heads. When they gave up ruffs and wore collars instead the men let their hair grow long and hang down on their shoulders in waves and curls. Sometimes a lock of hair was allowed to hang forward over one shoulder. In France this lock was called a 'cadenette' after a young man who first dressed his hair this way and braided the lock with 'favours'—ribbons, pearls or other little jewels, presented to him by his lady friends. In England the strand of hair was called a lovelock.

Some German folk-songs suggest that young men were in the habit of buying ribbons and other favours for themselves, and then pretending they had been given to them as love-tokens.

On their heads men wore hats of felt or beaver with wide brims, and trimmed with jewelled hat-bands and big ostrich plumes. Fashionable women wore similar hats and had curled

Hats of the early seventeenth century

fringes, sidecurls and their back hair dressed low. But at the same time a high crowned hat with a narrow, stiffer brim and trimmed with a plain band and buckle were worn by more serious people. Men at this time often had little pointed beards.

Fashionable women gave up wearing caps and veils or other head-dresses indoors, unless they were widows, when they wore a black cap which came to a point on the forehead, something like that worn by Mary, Queen of Scots, in the previous century. But women of the middle classes and lower wore white caps of a similar shape, or bonnets. Often, even out of doors, women now went bare-headed, or with nothing but a thin loose veil or a loose hood over their heads.

A great many women carried muffs to keep their hands warm, and in the summer, feather fans. Some pictures show them carrying both at the same time. They still carried masks, too, which they could put on when they did not want to be recognized, or to protect their faces from sun and wind. Some masks were small, only covering the eyes, some were big enough to cover the whole face.

A strange fashion that became increasingly popular was the patch—a little circle, or star, or other shaped piece of black velvet stuck on the face. Patches had been used in the sixteenth century—Shakespeare mentions them quite often—but it was in the 1640s that they began to get really popular. It is said that originally patches were used to hide pimples or other blemishes, but in the seventeenth century they were used because they were considered attractive, and they remained in fashion for a very long time.

Men and women still wore pouches or pockets attached to their belts. Men no longer carried daggers, but nearly every man wore a sword as a part of everyday dress. About this time men started to carry walking sticks—canes with round wooden or metal knobs.

At their best the clothes of the 1630s and 1640s were some of the most graceful and elegant there have ever been, and we in England know them well because of the pictures which the Flemish painter, Anthony Van Dyck, painted of Charles I and his family and the ladies and gentlemen of their court. Both men and women wore silk, satin and velvet, feathers, fine linen, beautiful lace, and many bows of ribbon, but they did not smother themselves with cloth of gold and gems to the same extent as the wealthy had done a few years earlier; neither did they stiffen and bombast their clothes into awkward and unnatural shapes. For a time clothes were looser, easier and far softer looking than they had been for a very long time.

But if the wealthy did not spend so much on gems, they often spent a fortune on lace. James I is said to have used twenty-five yards of lace for one ruff, and his wife eighteen yards, while their son, Charles I, paid £1,000 for lace alone in 1625, and another £1,500 in 1633. He is said to have bought a thousand yards of lace at one time for collars and cuffs and six hundred yards for night shirts.

Silk fabrics were easier to get than they had been earlier—though they were still expensive. For six hundred years after silkworms were brought to Constantinople the people of the Byzantine Empire alone possessed them. Then, in the twelfth century, the people of Sicily began to rear silkworms, and in the thirteenth people in various cities in Italy such as Florence and Milan. A century later France and Spain were competing, and soon after that the English began to wonder if it was not possible for them to cultivate this very profitable little insect and persuade it to produce silk for them. But the climate of England was not really suitable, and none of the early efforts was successful.

James I, in the early days of the seventeenth century, was particularly anxious to introduce this new industry into the country. So in 1608 he imported many thousands of mulberry trees (on the leaves of which silkworms feed) into England and had a great many of them planted near his palace of St. James's in London. The others were distributed over the country, with instructions about the breeding of silkworms. But the project was not a success, and just over forty years later, during the Commonwealth, the diarist John Evelyn speaks of the Mulberry Gardens as being 'the only place of refreshment about the town for persons of the best quality to be exceedingly cheated at'. James I's mulberry plantation had become a pleasure-garden, and the silkworms had disappeared.

Nevertheless, silk materials were woven in England from silk yarn imported, usually, from Italy, and they were not so rare and difficult to come by as they had been in the past. The persecution of the Protestants in Flanders and France caused many skilled Flemish and French weavers to settle in England.

CAVALIER ELEGANCE AND PURITAN PLAINNESS

There was a great deal of fighting in different parts of Europe during the seventeenth century. In England it was the century during which Englishmen fought against each other. Some, the Cavaliers, as the royalists were called, fought for King Charles I, and others, the Puritans, fought for parliament and Oliver Cromwell. As we all know, the Puritans won, and had the king

A Puritan couple

beheaded. For eleven years England was a Commonwealth, under Puritan rule.

Strict Puritans did not approve of men and women wearing rich fabrics, bright colours, feathers, bows, jewels, or in fact anything bright and gay. They themselves wore cloth doublets and breeches in sober, dark colours, without bows or other

M   177

ornaments except plain white collars, and stout, serviceable shoes, stockings and hats. They cut their hair short instead of letting it hang round their shoulders as the Cavaliers did, and for that reason they were called 'roundheads'. Puritan women wore plain full gowns of grey or some other sober coloured cloth, often tucked up over striped petticoats when they were working. Usually they wore plain white aprons over their dresses and white caps or bonnets on their heads.

Many men must have worn plain, simple clothes such as the leather suit which we are told George Fox, the founder of the Society of Friends, or Quakers, made for himself. He believed that the Lord had forbidden him 'to put off his hat to high or low'—in other words, he believed that he should treat all men as equals.

Although Cavaliers and Puritans felt so differently about clothes, it would be a mistake to think of *all* royalists as being clothed in rich materials, feathers and lace, and *all* parliamentarians as wearing drab coloured leather and cloth. There must have been many followers of Charles I who were not interested in dress and who wore plain, practical, simple clothes, and some parliamentarians who did not feel that silk, satin and bright colours were wicked.

All the same, during the eleven years of the Commonwealth life in England was very grave and serious, and people were not encouraged to waste time and money on frivolous things.

CHAPTER 17

Ribbons and Periwigs

As the seventeenth century advanced France began to take the lead in all matters of culture and taste. Louis XIV was king, and he was building his great palace at Versailles. The cleverest architects, artists, furniture-makers, carpet and tapestry weavers and garden designers were being employed to make the palace the finest and most wonderful in existence. The vast building, and the way in which it was equipped and decorated, were imitated by the great and wealthy all over Europe.

Elegant men and women everywhere tried to dress as French courtiers did, and clothes became more alike in every country in Europe than they had ever been before. 'Fashion' became very important, and everybody wanted to know as soon as possible exactly what was being worn in France. The shapes of such things as hats, collars and so on changed very rapidly, so that people who wanted to be considered up to date had to be constantly buying new clothes. Laws continued to be passed in Germany, Spain, England and France, and even in America, in attempts to stop extravagance and, more important, to make people dress according to the class to which they belonged.

In England, King Charles I's son returned from exile in France to be crowned Charles II. He and his family, and those who had shared his exile, were full of French ideas about clothes, and after the Restoration there was a very great change in the way people dressed, from the court downwards.

The makers of ribbon, lace and other decorative things must have had rather a difficult time during the Commonwealth, but now they had every reason for rejoicing. Men and women, as though they were tired to death of sober plain clothes, began to deck themselves with frills, puffs, bows, lace, ribbons, curls and feathers as they had never done before. Men's clothes, especially, were incredibly fussy. The fashionable court gentleman of the early 1660s wore a very short, straight, short-sleeved jacket, about to his waist, over a very full, blousy shirt, which puffed out over his breeches. The sleeves of the shirt were long and very full, and were sometimes tied in at the elbows with ribbons and finished at the wrists with wide lace-edged frills. The breeches worn with the little doublets were about knee-length and were very full and straight. Really fashionable men wore 'petticoat breeches', which were like short full skirts. Furious sermons were preached by clergymen in many pulpits against petticoat breeches, and many laws were passed against them in different parts of Europe, but they remained in fashion for many years.

A man of the 1660's

All breeches, whether 'petticoat' or not, were lavishly decorated with bunches of ribbon and with ribbon bows all the way round the waist and sometimes at the knees. In fact, the fashionable man put bunches of ribbon wherever he could find room for them—at wrist, elbow, shoulder, on his wide-brimmed, feathered hat, on his square-toed shoes, at his knee, and tied on the long cane which he carried in his hand.

We are told that in 1656 a really fashionable French gentleman would have five hundred to six hundred loops of ribbon scattered about over him, and expected to use something like three hundred yards of ribbon for the purpose.

John Evelyn, the English diarist, wrote in 1661: 'It was a fine silken thing which I spied th' other day through Westminster Hall, that had as much ribbon about him as would have plundered six shops, and set up twenty country pedlars; all his body was drest like a May-pole.'

More dignified, sober men wore knee-length, straight, coat-like garments with buttons all the way down the front, short sleeves with wide turn-back cuffs, and full breeches gathered in at the knee. Even they would probably have bows on their shoes. And by the sixties, too, a fashion had been adopted by almost all men of any standing that was to remain popular for over a hundred years—that of wearing wigs. The seventeenth century wig was generally made in the colours of natural hair— though no one pretended that the masses of curls that now hung about men's shoulders were really their own. At first human hair was used—fair hair being most in demand—but soon there was not enough human hair available to make all the wigs required, so goat or horse hair was used.

With the coming of wigs the wide collar was hidden, so a new kind of collar was introduced which was narrow at the back and shaped into a square in front. This collar, in the form of two white tabs hanging down below the chin, has survived until the present day in some forms of dress—such as that of the bluecoat boys and of some clergymen and lawyers.

The shoes worn by fashionable men in the second half of the seventeenth century were not trimmed with rosettes but with wide bows. A pair of shoes which were given as a wedding present to Louis XIV of France in 1660 had high red heels and were trimmed with bows sixteen inches wide. At the ends of the bows were smaller bows, each

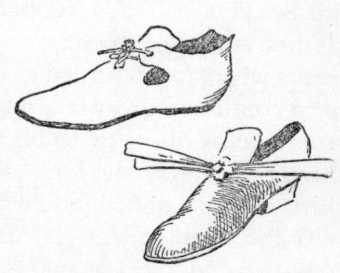

Late seventeenth century shoes

with a rosette in the centre. The king was delighted and declared he would never wear any other kind of shoe.

The clothes worn by people at court were, of course, imitated by others, as they always had been. This made many people very indignant. 'Display in dress has reached such a pitch', wrote a German writer, 'that it is impossible to distinguish artisan from nobleman and nobleman from prince.'

Some rulers tried to remedy this state of affairs. Maximilian of Bavaria divided his subjects into eight sections, from nobles down to peasants, and fixed precisely what clothes and trimmings the people in each section were to be allowed to wear. The Duke of Gotha divided his into six sections, and the same kind of thing was done in other places. All kinds of penalties were imposed on people who failed to dress in the clothes ordained for their particular section of the population. In Leipzig a Dr. Mostel, the son of a burgomaster, was fined for wearing black velvet for his wedding; at Dresden a lady was fined for wearing a velvet cap and a cloak trimmed with fur; at Nuremberg a printer was fined again and again because his wife was too finely dressed—and their dog wore a silver collar!

The importation of foreign goods was forbidden in many places, but somehow French finery continued to pour in, and was bought and worn by all who could afford it, in spite of the regulations.

All the same, the extraordinary clothes worn by fashionable men were no good at all for men who had any active work to do. Soldiers naturally adopted rather plainer, more practical, clothes, and sometimes they went on wearing these simpler garments when they returned to ordinary life. Louis XIV is said to have continued to wear a military type of coat after returning from one of his visits to his army, and it is said to have been through him that the long slit in the coat sleeve, showing the shirt, was abandoned. Some rulers tried really seriously to simplify the costume worn by themselves and their courtiers, and to put an end to extravagance.

During the month of October 1666 a change came over court fashions in England for which King Charles II seems to have been responsible. Two men who were writing diaries at the time, John Evelyn and Samuel Pepys, both tell us something about the change, and Evelyn suggests that he himself may have had something to do with it. He writes, on October 18th:

'To Court. It being the first time his Majesty put himself solemnly into the Eastern fashion of vest, changeing doublet, stiff collar, bands and cloake, into a comely vest, after the Persian mode with girdle or straps, and shoe strings and garters into bouckles, of which some were set with precious stones, resolving never to alter it, and to leave the French mode, which had hitherto obtained to our great expence and reproch. Upon which divers courtiers and gentlemen gave his Majesty gold by way of wager that he would not persist in this resolution. I had sometime before presented an invective against that unconstancy, and our so much affecting the French fashion, to his Majesty, in which I took occasion to describe the comlinesse and usefulnesse of the Persian clothing, in the very same manner his Majesty now clad himselfe. This pamphlet I intitl'd "Tyrannus, or the Mode", and gave it to his Majesty to reade. I do not impute to this discourse the change which soon happen'd, but it was an identity that I could not but take notice of.'

On October 30th Evelyn writes:

'To London to our office, and now I had on the vest and surcoat or tunic as 'twas called, after his Majesty had brought the whole Court to it. It was comely and manly habit, too good to hold, it being impossible for us in good ernest to leave the Monsieurs vanities long.'

Samuel Pepys mentions the king's new clothes on October 13th, when he says he visited the Duke of York (the king's brother, who later became King James II) and says: '. . . so I stood and saw him dress himself and try on his vest, which is the king's new fashion and he will be in it for good and all on Monday next, and the whole court; it is a fashion, the king says, he will never change.'

Two days later, Pepys writes: 'This day the King begins to put on his vest, and I did see several persons of the House of Lords and Commons too, great courtiers who are in it; being a long cassocke close to the body, of black cloth, and pinked with white silk under it, and a coat over it, and the legs ruffled with black riband like a pigeon's leg; and upon the whole I wish the King may keep it, for it is a very fine and handsome garment.'

By November 4th, Pepys can write: 'My taylor's man brings my vest home, and coat to wear with it, and belt and silver-hilted sword; so I rose and dressed myself, and I like myself mightily in it, and so do my wife ... it being very cold, to White Hall, and was mighty fearfull of an ague, my vest being new and thin, and the coat cut not to meet before, upon my vest.'

On November 12th, alas, he records: 'Going to Sir R. Viner's I did get such a splash and spots of dirt upon my new vest, that I was out of countenance to be seen in the street.'

Such disasters must have been fairly common in those days of undrained and often unpaved streets.

At that time France and England were on very bad terms, and Louis XIV of France thought of an ingenious way of discrediting Charles II of England. Pepys tells how he heard about it. On November 22nd he writes: 'Mr. Batelier tells me the news how the King of France hath, in defiance to the King of England, caused all his footmen to be put into vests, and that the noblemen of France will do the like; which, if true, is the greatest indignity ever done by one Prince to another and would excite a stone to be revenged. ... This makes me mighty merry, it being an ingenious kind of affront; but yet makes me angry to see that the King of England is become so little as to have the affront offered him.'

Whether or not Charles II continued to wear his new-style vest and coat in their original form seems doubtful, but there is no doubt at all that long straight coats sometimes, but not always, with a vest (or waistcoat) under them, became universal for men during the last quarter of the seventeenth century. Not that they were always any less extravagant than earlier clothes. In France gold and silver embroidery had been forbidden since 1633, but Louis XIV got over this difficulty by ordaining that certain people to whom he gave a royal warrant might wear a blue coat lined with red and embroidered all over in silver and gold. The wearer of this garment had the right to go everywhere with the king without being specially invited, and the number of men thus privileged was restricted to about sixty. To be included was regarded as the greatest possible honour.

The word 'vest' was used to describe the garment that was

Straight coat—Charles II's time

later called a 'waistcoat'. In the seventeenth century the waistcoat was usually as long as the coat, or, at first, a few inches longer, and both, at first, were straight and not shaped in at all at the waist. The sleeves of the coat were short, those of the waistcoat a little longer and turned back over the coat sleeves. Neither had collars, since the periwig covered the neck and shoulders and men began to wear cravats—strips of fine linen with lace ends—twisted round their necks and tied in a bow in front. In order to help English lacemakers, the importing of foreign lace into England was forbidden in 1662—but Charles II and James II seem, all the same, to have had very large quan-

Slightly shaped coat—late seventeenth century

tities of Venetian and Belgian lace, and smugglers of lace did a brisk trade.

Towards the end of the century coats were shaped in at the waist, with wide skirts and longer sleeves, and with very wide cuffs. They were often worn unbuttoned to show the long waist-coat, which, in its turn, was often only buttoned at the waist, so as to show the shirt. In a letter which has survived since 1680 a boy writes to his mother: 'I do hope you will consider to buy me some good shirts, or else some sort of waistcoat, for it is not fashionable for any gentleman to go buttoned up either winter or summer.'

Men still wore ruffles at their wrists and sometimes sashes round their waists. But the rosettes and bows on the shoes disappeared, to be replaced by buckles, and the shoes themselves had big tongues which came high over the wearer's instep. The wide brims of the hats were often turned up, or 'cocked', in various ways, and often the hats were carried under the arm so that they should not disturb the carefully arranged periwig.

Gloves were not much worn by men at this time, but they often carried muffs, which were sometimes suspended round their necks by velvet ribbons. Fashionable men, too, wore corsets.

For the first time men were supplied with something that has been an essential part of man's costume ever since—real pockets. At first the pockets were very low down—only a few inches above the hem of the long coat—but later they were put a little higher. They nearly always had flaps that could be buttoned down over the opening.

Ladies during the second half of the seventeenth century wore dresses cut very low at the neck—a fashion that was, of course, denounced by the Church and forbidden by various governments, all without the slightest effect. With plain dresses the opening was often filled in with a folded kerchief, or the higher neck of the chemise. Sometimes a fitted lace collar called a bertha outlined the edge of the low round-necked bodices, and frills of lace hung from the elbow-length sleeves. Lace aprons were worn, too, and sometimes lace gloves or mittens.

The close-fitting bodices were still brought down to a point at the waist in front, and were laced up with cords or ribbons either in front or at the back. Often bodices and skirts were of different materials and different colours. The skirts were long and full, and under them country women might wear a red flannel or striped petticoat, while the wealthier woman would wear one of silk or satin richly decorated.

In the sixties women in England began to wear a special outfit for riding (they had never done so before). It was an imitation of the riding clothes worn by men. The coat was close-fitting at the waist, with wide skirts and sleeves with huge cuffs, and at their throats they wore cravats and on their heads periwigs and cocked hats. They continued, of course, to wear their full skirts and many petticoats. This new fashion shocked many people. Pepys saw it for the first time on 11th June 1666:

Lady—second half of seventeenth century

'Walking in the galleries at White Hall, I find the Ladies of honour dressed in their riding garbs, with coats and doublets with deep skirts, just, for all the world, like mine; and buttoned their doublets up the breast, with periwigs and with hats; so that only for a long petticoat dragging under their men's coats, nobody could take them for women in any point whatever; which was an odde sight, and a sight did not please me.'

But whether men approved or not, women found the masculine-looking riding-coats comfortable and practical and continued to wear them—and have, to some extent, done so ever since, though the riding-habit has, of course, changed in detail from time to time.

Pepys writes rather sadly on 18th August 1660: 'Towards Westminster by water. I landed my wife at Whitefriars with £5 to buy her a petticoat, and my father persuaded her to buy a most fine cloth, of 26s. a yard, and a rich lace, that the petticoat will come to £5; but she doing it very innocently, I could not be angry.'

On the following day he writes: 'Home to dinner, where my wife had on her new petticoat that she bought yesterday, which indeed is a very fine cloth and a fine lace; but that being of a light colour, and the lace all silver, it makes no great shew.'

So completely had fashions changed by this time that when a Portuguese princess arrived, to become the wife of Charles II, the Spanish clothes which she and her ladies wore—the huge farthingale and high, tight bodice—horrified English people. Pepys, who saw them on 30th May 1662, described them as 'monstrous'.

Pepys often refers to his wife's clothes and what they looked like and how much they cost him—but he refers far more often to his own. He was keenly interested in dress—partly perhaps because he was the son of a tailor—and as he gradually became richer and more important so he gradually spent more money on clothes and became more concerned about being in the fashion.

In August 1662 he records that he has called at his father's 'to change my long black cloak for a short one (long cloaks being now quite out)'. He tells us when his 'fine camlet cloak with gold buttons' is sent home, and his 'new silk suit', which will cost him a great deal of money. 'I pray God to make me able to pay for it,' he writes. When, ten days later, he puts on the silk suit to go to a wedding he confides to his diary that it is the first silk suit he ever wore. But there were to be many more, and he never fails to tell us about them and the price ($£24$ or so) which he had to pay for them. He describes the gold or silver buttons, and the gold lace frills at the wrists, and is immensely proud of them.

A few months after wearing his first silk suit Pepys writes: 'This is the first day that ever I saw my wife wear black patches since we were married.' He does not say whether or not he liked them, but since they were fashionable he probably approved. Patches had been fashionable on the continent for a long time. A traveller reports seeing them in Berlin in 1616. But they do not appear to have been worn very much in England until 1650, when a writer describes seeing them and says that ladies, besides wearing patches on their faces in the form of stars, crescent moons and so on, also stuck on their foreheads patches shaped like a coach and horses.

Pepys was very proud of his wife and liked her to look nice and to hear her praised and admired. On one occasion he writes in his diary: 'To Westminster Hall, where I purposely took my wife well dressed into the Hall to see and be seen.'

In May 1663 Pepy's diary tells us something of his feelings about the new periwigs (which was the English form of the French word 'perruque') that so many men were beginning to wear. On May 9th he writes: 'At Mr. Jarvas's, my old barber. I did try two or three borders and periwigs, meaning to wear one; and yet I have no stomach for it, but that the pains of keeping my hair clean is so great. He trimmed me, and at last I parted, but my mind was almost altered from my first purpose, from the trouble that I foresee will be in wearing them also.'

He has no more to say about periwigs until August 21st, when he writes that his brother Tom, who evidently worked with their father, the tailor, had been to see him. 'We did resolve of putting me into a better garbe, and, among other things, to have a good velvet cloak—that is, of cloth, lined with velvet, and other things modish, and a perruque, and so he and my wife out to buy me velvet.'

RIBBONS AND PERIWIGS

On August 29th he is able to write: 'This morning was brought home my new velvet cloak—that is, lined with velvet, a good cloth the outside—the first that ever I had in my life, and I pray God it may not be too soon now that I begin to wear it.' On the 30th he took his wife to his periwig maker's to see the new periwig 'which she said she liked'.

But that night he did his accounts and was grieved to find that he had spent £67 on clothes—£12 on his wife and £55 on himself. He had bought two periwigs, one costing £3 and the other £2, and various shirts, hats, gowns, etc. 'But', he writes, 'I hope I shall have more comfort, labour to get more, and with better success than when for want of clothes I was forced to sneak like a beggar.'

Periwigs had been worn in France for quite a long time. As early as 1613 travellers had seen them in Paris, and in 1624 King Louis XIII, who had gone bald, started wearing one. But Pepys, in not yet having worn one before 1663, was not behind the English fashion. On November 2nd, three days after showing his new one to his wife he mentions that he has heard the Duke of York say that he is going to wear a periwig, and that he has heard rumours that the king will also.

On November 3rd Pepys writes: 'By and by comes Chapman, the periwig-maker, and upon my liking it, without more ado I went up and there he cut off my haire, which went a little to my heart at present to part with it; but, it being over, and my periwig on, I paid him £3 for it, and away went he, with my own haire, to make up another of; and I, by and by, went abroad, after I had caused all my maids to look upon it; and they conclude it do become me, though Jane was mightily troubled for my parting of my own haire, and so was Besse.'

A great many men about this time must have experienced Pepys's misgivings over parting with their own hair and adopting a periwig. They must have shared, too, the feelings of shyness and embarrassment that Pepys certainly felt on first walking abroad and meeting his friends in his new adornment. But having once adopted the fashion it was many years before men gave it up again.

Periwigs were abused, of course, and for years the clergy, both Catholic and Protestant, would not wear them. But they took to them in the end—and then continued to wear them long after everyone else had given them up.

In some places periwigs were forbidden for a number of years, but the authorities everywhere had to give way in the end. In Venice, for instance, the first periwig was worn in 1668 by a Venetian who had brought it from France. But the state forbade its citizens to wear such things, and it was not until several years later that they gave permission for a small periwig to be worn. Even then many old-fashioned people fought against what they must have regarded as a ridiculous fashion. One man, in his will, disinherited his son if he continued to wear a periwig, and another Venetian managed to get together a company of about two hundred and fifty men, all of whom swore they would never wear periwigs. Whether they all kept their word we do not know, but their leader certainly did. He died in 1757 without ever having worn anything but his own hair. But such people were exceptional, and long before the end of the seventeenth century nearly all men of any standing anywhere were wearing periwigs.

Periwigs had to be carefully arranged and looked after, and men used to take combs to the opera and other places with them so that they could comb and tidy their curls, which were usually arranged in three masses, one hanging down the back and one over each shoulder.

Since periwigs could be very expensive—as much as fifty guineas—thieves thought out all kinds of clever ways of stealing them. One way was to conceal a small boy in a large basket which a man carried up on his shoulder, as bakers carried their bread baskets in those days. The man walked along a crowded street, and when someone wearing a fine looking periwig came along an accomplice knocked against him and the small boy in the basket knocked his hat off. As the gentleman bent to pick up his hat the boy hastily pulled off his periwig, and the false baker dashed away round a corner, where the boy jumped out ef the basket, tucked the wig in his satchel and went off. If the unfortunate owner of the wig came round the corner all he saw was a baker with one or two loaves doing his rounds, and an innocent-looking boy on the way to school.

Of course, this trick did not always work, and gentlemen in periwigs soon began to give bakers a wide berth. Soon genuine bakers began to carry their baskets on their arms, or sloping over their backs, so that people could see that they were carrying only loaves.

In 1684 Guardsmen in England were ordered 'to tye the hair back with a ribbon', so that it should not blow across their faces and into their eyes when they were firing. By the end of the century the hair was being tucked into bags which men wore hanging down their backs.

Women, as a rule, wore their own hair in natural looking ringlets and curls—though they were sometimes wired to make them stand away from the face—and sometimes they wore posies of flowers, bunches of ribbons or strings of pearls in their hair. Country women and simple housewives still often wore caps or bonnets.

But about 1690 there was a change. Women began to pile their hair up high over their foreheads, enclose it at the back in a close cap, and place in front a high structure of lace or lawn, pleated, starched and wired to keep it in place. This head-dress was called a 'fontange' (after a lady at the French court called the Duchesse de Fontange), or a 'commode', or even simply a 'tower'. It remained fashionable for about thirty years, in spite of furious abuse and ridicule. Louis XIV, at whose court it originated, is said to have got very tired of it, but even he could not persuade women to give it up. A German clergyman disliked this head-dress so much that

A fontange and hood

N   193

he even went so far as to snatch the fontange from a lady's head as he passed her.

Sometimes black velvet ribbons or long lappets of lace or lawn hung down the wearer's back from either side of the cap. When they went out women might wear a large hood which covered the fontange, or an extra large shawl might be draped over it and round the shoulders.

Late seventeenth century woman

By this time—the 1690s—fashionable ladies wore their outer dresses very long so that they trailed on the ground at the back. They were almost always open up the front and the two edges were often pinned back. But now women began to pile the dress up at the back to make what is called a 'bustle', and sometimes they wore a wire support under the piled-up fulness to increase the effect.

Unfortunately neither they nor their menfolk gave as much attention to cleanliness as we should think necessary. Washing was thought to be unhealthy, and a French writer of 1640 lays down the rule that 'an occasional bath should be taken, the hands washed daily, and the face every day or so'. But it is to be feared that many people did not go even as far as this. The hands of Queen Christina of Sweden, which were very beautiful, could hardly be seen for dirt, so we are told, and a gentleman who sent some soap from Italy to a lady, had to tell her very carefully how to use it. Men and women changed their under-linen only once a month.

CHAPTER 18

Coats and Waistcoats Come to Stay

During the eighteenth century the influence of the French court on the fashions of Europe became stronger than ever. Whatever was worn at Versailles was copied first by society in Paris and then by the well-to-do people in the rest of Europe. And the fashions worn by the aristocracy worked down until, in a simpler form and in cheaper materials, they were worn by the humblest everywhere.

London women were kept informed about the changes in French fashions in this way. Towards the end of the seventeenth century Paris began to send over every month large dolls, or models, dressed in the very latest style. There was big Pandora, who was dressed in the very smartest clothes, and little Pandora, who wore a négligé, by which was meant the kind of dress one would wear at home or among one's friends. Later Pandora's sisters began regular visits to other countries—Russia, Germany and Italy.

The bodices of ladies' dresses were always tight-fitting, and were usually long-waisted and came down to a point in front. They had low necks, square or round, and short sleeves. Sometimes a big soft collar called a fichu was draped round the neck and crossed over in front. The bodices were often laced up over an under-bodice, as they had been before, or they might have an embroidered panel up the front, or be trimmed with horizontal strips of lace or braid, or have several little bows one above the other.

From early childhood girls wore tight corsets with a straight metal rod up the front.

About 1710 fashionable women, who had been free from

195

farthingales, or hoops, for nearly a century (except in Spain) took to wearing them again. At first the hoop, like the Spanish farthingale of the mid-sixteenth century, was bell-shaped. It was made by stitching five or more circles of, at first, metal or wood, and later, whalebone, to a stiff petticoat. Some hoops were of moderate size, but others were simply enormous so that the wearers took up a great deal of room.

Eighteenth century lady

At Versailles a rule was made that when the court attended the theatre chairs on either side of the queen must be left empty, so that she should not be hidden by the hoops of the royal princesses. Then the princesses demanded that they should have empty chairs between them and the duchesses, and the duchesses insisted that they should likewise be separated from the countesses, and so on. Finally it was settled that princesses and duchesses should be separated, but that ladies of lower rank must manage to fit their hoops in as best they could.

Soon women of all classes were wearing hoops—though attempts were made, as usual, to keep the lower classes from wearing them, and in some places women and girls who appeared in them were fined. Other laws about dress were enforced in different places. In Bavaria, for instance, women below a certain rank were not allowed to wear embroidered caps, and on New Year's Day in 1750 officials waited at the doors of all churches and roughly snatched such caps from their wearers' heads.

In the eighteenth century English people did not go to the seaside every year as so many of us do to-day, but they did, whenever they could, go to Bath to drink and bathe in the medicinal waters that bubble up out of the earth there. But they did not go only for their health. There were concerts, balls, assemblies and all kinds of social functions, and people attended them partly to admire and envy each other's clothes, and to show off their own.

For some years in the early part of the eighteenth century the Master of Ceremonies at Bath was a man who had a real genius for organizing things. His name was Nash, and 'Beau Nash' as he was called became an absolute dictator where fashions and manners were concerned. He made his own rules, and his influence was so great that people were perfectly willing to obey them. At that time it was fashionable for ladies to wear fancy aprons of lace or some other delicate fabric with their smartest clothes. Nash was one of the people who disliked this fashion. One day when the Duchess of Queensberry arrived at a Bath Assembly wearing a lace apron worth two hundred guineas he tore it off and threw it in a corner. Nash's power and influence were so great that the Duchess appears to have accepted his reproof quite meekly.

An eighteenth century
sacque gown

197

One very popular kind of dress in the eighteenth century was called a sacque. The skirt part of it was wide and full, as usual, and the bodice was cut to fit closely in front. But at the back the fulness was gathered or pleated into the neck and hung straight down to the ground. Later the pleats were stitched down as far as the waist. Ladies wearing dresses like these appear in pictures by Watteau and other artists of the time, and some of the actual dresses themselves, and other interesting eighteenth-century clothes, can be seen in the Victoria and Albert Museum in London.

For the first few years of the eighteenth century fashionable ladies at the French court continued to wear the fontange, sometimes as much as two foot high. Louis XIV disliked it and tried, to everybody's indignation, to prohibit it. The ladies would not give it up, and they went on wearing it until 1714, when, so it is said, the English Duchess of Shrewsbury appeared at the French court without a fontange, and was complimented by the king.

After that time women began to arrange their hair close to

Women's caps—eighteenth century

the head, often with bunches of long or short curls at the back. Sometimes, for special occasions, they decorated it in front with little wreaths of flowers, or other ornaments, and most women, indoors, wore little caps of lace or lawn. The bigger cap which covered the head and had a frill all the way round, which we call a mob cap, came in about this time and was worn for many years, especially, later, by country girls.

When they went out many women put on a low-crowned, wide-brimmed hat of felt or straw. They might wear the hat over their caps. Straw hats had been made and worn by country people for years, but in the eighteenth century fashionable people took to them—though they liked them to be beautifully made from the best possible straw. They often came from Leghorn in Italy. But English straw hats became popular, too, and

Women's hats in the eighteenth century

hat-making developed into a big industry in such centres as Dunstable and Luton. The hats were made by women and children in their own cottages. They were, of course, sewn by hand. Little children began plaiting straw at four years old.

Besides caps and straw hats, hoods, either separate or attached to cloaks, were still worn a great deal.

So far as men were concerned, the coats and waistcoats which they had begun to wear in the last quarter of the seventeenth century had come to stay, and are still with us, though in a very different form.

At first the skirt part of the knee-length coat was often very wide and was stiffened with horsehair to make it stand out. Cuffs were bigger than ever. The coats were still provided with buttons all the way down, but only one or two, sometimes over the chest, sometimes at the waist, were ever done up, or were even meant to do up. The vest, or waistcoat, was generally now

Early eighteenth century man

a little shorter than the coat, and was usually lighter in colour, or made of some gaily flowered or embroidered material. Like the coat, it was now given pockets, in which the elegant wearer could keep his snuff-box and his lace-edged handkerchief.

Gentlemen wore breeches of black velvet, or of light-coloured satin. Countrymen, middle-class townsmen and men of simple tastes wore plain, hard-wearing cloth.

The toes of shoes now became round instead of square, and the tongues were not so long as they had been—though buckles became very large. Until about 1715 men went on wearing the huge periwig. After that the wig-makers began to take the hair back from the face in various ways, either by tying it back with a ribbon, arranging it in a plait down the back, or packing it into a black silk bag which was then drawn up with a string and finished with a black bow. In front they drew the hair back from the forehead and arranged it at the sides in a puff or in a number of horizontal curls over the ears.

Some men, of course, grew their own hair, pomaded and powdered it, and arranged it as the wig-makers did. Servants and simpler people let it rest naturally on their shoulders, without powder. Soldiers and sailors wore pigtails down their backs and old-fashioned people went on wearing full wigs. In time, however, the full-bottomed wig was worn only by learned men

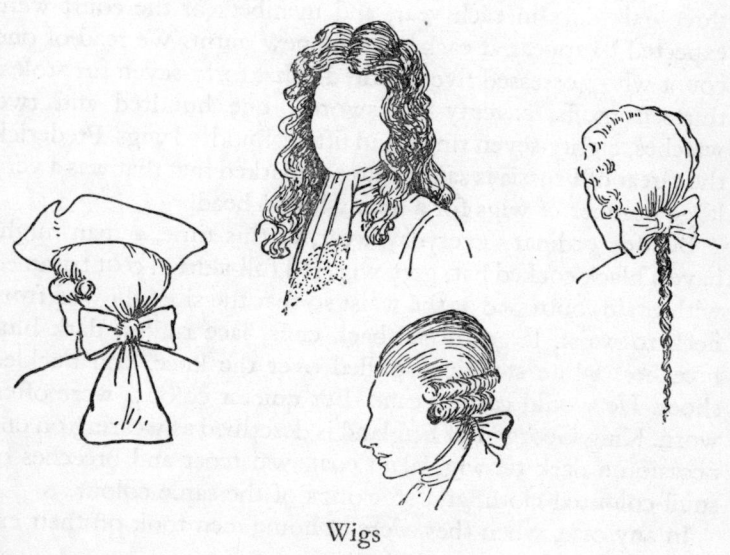

Wigs

such as judges. Gradually different shaped wigs came to be associated with different professions or trades, or with the wearer's position in life. A doctor or clergyman did not wear the same kind of wig as a coachman, or an army officer the same as a country gentleman.

By the early 1700s nearly all men and women wore their hair or their periwigs powdered. The powdering had to be done very evenly, and wealthy people had special closets provided in their houses for the purpose. They would sit with their faces in a paper bag while a servant or barber tossed powder against the ceiling, so that it fell on the head in an even cloud.

Fashionable men also used face powder, rouge and patches, just as ladies did. It was not necessary that the make-up should look natural—in fact, in France it was considered to be in bad taste if it did.

The clothes worn by society men were still very elaborate and costly, and they had to have a great many of them. We hear of men at some of the courts of Europe who were expected to change their suits three times a day; at others no gentleman might appear twice in the same suit; at one there were thirty-three gala days in each year, and members of the court were expected to appear at each one in a new outfit. We read of one count who possessed five hundred suits, forty-seven fur stoles, thirteen muffs, seventy-five swords, one hundred and two watches, eighty-seven rings, and fifteen hundred wigs. Frederick the Great of Prussia is said to have remarked that that was a very large number of wigs for a man with no head!

But for ordinary everyday wear, at this time, a man might have a black cocked hat, grey wig, red full-skirted coat trimmed with braid, buttoned at the waist so that the shirt showed from neck to waist, large turned-back cuffs, lace ruffles, dark blue breeches, white stockings pulled over the knee, and buckled shoes. He would carry a cane. But quieter colours were often worn. King George I of England is described as wearing on one occasion a dark tie-wig, plain coat, waistcoat and breeches of snuff-coloured cloth, and stockings of the same colour.

In any case, when they were at home men took off their expensive suits and their periwigs and put on a garment like a modern dressing-gown, and tied a scarf round their heads or put on a close-fitting cap. There are a number of eighteenth-century portraits of well-known men showing them in this informal outfit, and several artists painted portraits of themselves wearing it.

Nearly all men wore hats of which the wide brims were turned up, or 'cocked' to make them three-cornered in shape. They were worn with one corner facing forwards.

The lace-edged cravat gradually disappeared, and a plain muslin band called a stock was often placed round the neck instead. Sometimes a narrow black ribbon was placed over the stock. A jabot, or frill, was then often placed down the front

A riding coat

of the shirt, to froth out between the two sides of the waistcoat.

Out of doors men wore long cloaks with one end thrown over the left shoulder, or across the face if they did not want to be recognized. In England men sometimes wore, for riding, overcoats which were similar in shape to their ordinary coats, but bigger and of thicker material. About 1725 these riding coats were introduced into France, but were worn only for travelling. No fashionable gentleman would wear one in Paris or at court.

Coats with full, stiffened skirts were not very suitable for riding or fighting, so soldiers wore neater and closer-fitting clothes. Their waistcoats were shorter than those worn by civilians, and they wore narrower cuffs and no wrist ruffles. At first they turned up the skirts of their coats and buttoned them at the back when they were riding, but before long the skirts were cut away from the front, and were only long at the back, something like the tail-coats that men still wear for evening dress. The two buttons which had been used for fastening back the skirts were still placed in position although they were no longer necessary —and they still are. The huge cuffs became narrower, and the buttons and buttonholes which had previously buttoned them back to the sleeve were still put on as decoration. After a time the cuff itself disappeared, and the close-fitting sleeve was buttoned up at the back. The coats men wear to-day still have buttons at the back of the sleeve, although sleeves are always wide enough to draw over the hand.

These buttons at the back of the coat and on the sleeves are examples of the way in which something that was once necessary continues to appear on our clothes long after it has ceased to be used, and most people have forgotten that it ever served any useful purpose. Another example is the wide collar on a sailor's jacket, which was originally introduced to protect his coat from the grease from his queue, or pigtail.

Soon men began to wear the military type of suit for ordinary everyday wear, And during the eighteenth century, too, the wearing of uniforms began—that is to say, the soldiers of different countries were distinguished from each other by the colour of their coats, the shape of their hats and so on, and different regiments in the same army might be distinguished by various details. Certain rulers—Frederick the Great was one of the first—began to wear military uniforms for ordinary daily wear.

Some rulers, too, in an attempt to curb the dreadful extrava-

An eighteenth century cutaway coat

gance of the time, had special clothes, or uniforms, designed for their ladies and gentlemen to wear at court. At one court men were expected to wear green coats with white lapels and white waistcoats. At another, ladies wore red gowns trimmed with gold lace.

The breeches which gentlemen wore with the short waistcoats and cut-away coats must, if a man wanted to look really smart, fit very tightly and smoothly. Often the wearers were afraid to sit down for fear of splitting their breeches, which had to be held up by two servants when their masters forced themselves into them. Sometimes a man ordered two pairs of breeches with a suit—one pair in which he could and one in which he could not sit down.

In time, as men began to wear simpler, plainer clothes, embroidery, silk and satin were reserved for court dress or special occasions. Ordinary clothes and hats were often trimmed with gold braid. But some men then started to decorate their coats with buttons as big as five-shilling-pieces, which were often so costly that the suit was as expensive as the embroidered ones had been. Some such buttons were miniature pictures under glass. A Comte d'Artois is said to have worn watches on his coat in place of buttons—whilst still, so his friends said, having no idea of time.

Embroidered waistcoats lingered on even after coats became plain. Sometimes they were embroidered with scenes illustrating operas and plays, or with such strange subjects as green monkeys carrying silver parasols.

CHAPTER 19

Hoops and Panniers

While, during the eighteenth century, the clothes worn by men tended to become simpler, those worn by really fashionable women after about 1760 were more fantastic than they had been for years. Skirts spread out to an enormous width at the wearer's hips, and the upper skirt was often drawn up in great puffs and flounces. Bows and ribbons and frills were everywhere.

But the most surprising thing was the style of hair-dressing. Women began to dress their hair very high. Among women such as those at the French court of Louis XVI and Marie

Late eighteenth century
hair styles

Antoinette, and the people who imitated them, the hair was drawn up as much as three feet above the wearer's head over pads or wire frames, was thickly coated with pomade to make it stay in place, was then smothered with powder, and finally decorated with all kinds of things such as baskets of fruit, bunches of flowers, feathers, and even such outlandish things as a ship in full sail or a model of a coach and horses.

There are many humorous eighteenth-century drawings in existence showing ladies unable to pass through doors because of their towering head-dresses, or sitting in sedan chairs from which the roofs have had to be removed, or kneeling on the floors of coaches because their heads were too high for them to sit on the seats. A baroness writing at the time states that a fashionable lady's chin should be just about midway between her toes and the top of her hair.

This elaborate hair-dressing had to be done by experienced hairdressers. Marie Antoinette's hairdresser was named Leonard Autier, and he became famous. Whatever style of hair-dressing he designed for the Queen was immediately imitated by other women. One lady paid her hairdresser an enormous sum yearly on condition that he supplied her with a new style every day. But few people even in society had their hair dressed daily. The outlandish styles took a very long time to do, so once up the hair was left for as long as possible—sometimes several weeks—before it was taken down again. By that time it was very dirty and unhealthy. Women slept as best they could after encasing their heads in a big bag like a pillow case.

Although most men by this time were wearing small, neat periwigs (or perukes, as they were then more often called) there were some who imitated the women and wore powdered wigs that were a foot high. In particular the Macaronis, who were members of a London club, gave a great deal of attention to their appearance, and tried to make themselves conspicuous by wearing clothes more striking than those worn by other men. Perched on top of their lofty wigs they wore tiny tricorn hats, and on their legs they wore striped stockings over false calves made of cork fastened on to their legs to make them look a good shape. They wore corsets too, of course, just as all women and a great many other men did, and they used paint and powder, scent, lace handkerchiefs and beribboned canes.

But the Macaronis, and the women with three-foot high head-dresses, were exceptional, and the simpler clothes worn by ordinary men and women were graceful and picturesque.

We in England like to think of eighteenth-century men and women in beautifully proportioned houses full of graceful furniture designed by such men as Sheraton, Hepplewhite and Chippendale. And we picture elegantly dressed gentlemen, in embroidered silk and satin, taking pinches of snuff from gold, silver and enamelled snuff-boxes, while their ladies poured tea and coffee from silver pots into dainty porcelain cups, which had probably come from China, and they all discussed the pictures being painted by Gainsborough and Reynolds, the latest play, the acting of David Garrick, the learning of Dr. Johnson, or the last season at Bath.

But this, of course, is only one side of the picture. At the same time John Wesley was riding ceaselessly about the country preaching to eager congregations of poor people, and he, like thousands of other men, wore plain, practical, hard-wearing clothes of woollen cloth. And the people he preached to were often hard put to it to provide themselves with clothes at all, and many of them had probably never heard of Reynolds or Garrick, or so much as seen a Hepplewhite chair or a Chippendale bookcase.

Among the famous men of the day there were a great many who, although they dressed in the style of their time (as we nearly all do in any period), cared nothing at all for silks and satins and fine embroidery.

A great eighteenth-century sculptor named Joseph Nollekens made an enormous fortune, but he was rather a miser, and he certainly spent as little as possible on clothes. Nevertheless, he bought himself a purple velvet suit and some fine lace ruffles when he was studying in Rome as a young man. He smuggled the lace home to England inside a hollow bust of Laurence Sterne which he had modelled in Rome.

At this time immense sums were still being spent on lace, and everything possible was done to encourage and help the lace-makers of various countries by banning the import of lace from other countries and confiscating it when it was smuggled in. In England, three days before the marriage of King George III's sister, Augusta, to the Duke of Brunswick, customs men went to the workshops of the court dressmakers and took away every garment trimmed with foreign lace. Brussels lace was the most valued, partly because the Netherlands produced the whitest and finest thread, but chiefly because the lace-makers were so expert and did such beautiful work. Venice was famous for lace, and still is, yet when the Doge's son was married in 1770 the gowns of all the ladies present were trimmed with Brussels lace, and the altar cloth alone was made of local lace.

We hear of an eighteenth-century bride who spent £5,000 on lace alone for her trousseau. Brides often gave lace ruffles as gifts to their bridegrooms, for every gentleman, however poor he might be, and however shabby his clothes, liked his lace ruffles to be of the very finest.

Nollekens wore his ruffles and his velvet suit on his wedding day in 1772, with a pair of stockings with blue and white stripes, a sword, cocked hat and bag wig—and he continued to wear the same clothes to Royal Academy dinners, and when he attended court, for fifty years afterwards. At his death he left only one other coat, two shirts, three pairs of stockings, one pair of breeches (or 'small clothes' as they were called at this time) two waistcoats, and two odd shoes.

We have a description of Nollekens' bride on her wedding-day, from which we learn that she wore a sacque and petticoat of exquisitely brocaded white silk with a deep pointed stomacher, at the lower part of which was a large diamond pin holding in place a point-lace apron which she wore because it had belonged to her mother, although it was not really fashionable then. Her sleeves were close-fitting to below the elbow, below which were three wide point-lace ruffles. At her breast was a large bow of ribbon, and a bouquet of rose-buds, and three rows of pearls were round her neck. Her beautiful auburn hair which, we are told, she never disguised by the use of powder, was arranged over a cushion to a considerable height, with large round curls at the side, the whole being surmounted by a small point-lace cap. She wore shoes with heels three and a half inches high.

A mid-eighteenth century woman

But, like her husband, Mrs. Nollekens spent very little money on clothes after her wedding, for she became as great a miser as he was.

Dr. Johnson was quite indifferent to clothes. He wore a rather full wig, though, as we are told that he frequently singed it when he was peering at books by candle-light with his short-sighted eyes, it cannot have looked very smart. Nollekens, when he modelled a bust of Dr. Johnson, insisted on depicting him without his wig, but as though he had thick heavy locks of his own, which he had not. Nollekens said this would make the Doctor look more like a poet of Ancient Greece or Rome, but Johnson was annoyed and said that in his opinion people should be portrayed in pictures and statues as they appeared in company.

Artists at that time often represented great men dressed as though they were Greeks or Romans, and when Benjamin West painted the Death of Wolfe and insisted on depicting the characters in the clothes they actually wore at the time, there was a great uproar and many people disapproved.

One thing that would strike us if we could return to the eighteenth century would be the fact that men and women, even when they were finely dressed, were still not at all particular about cleanliness. A writer named John Thomas Smith, who wrote a biography of Nollekens, tells us that the sculptor was fond of going to the Opera, when he had to wear his purple suit, his sword and bag wig. But the Opera House was burnt down, and performances were given after that in another building, and the rules about dress were relaxed. One day Boswell, the biographer of Dr. Johnson, met the sculptor and exclaimed loudly, 'Why, Nollekens, how dirty you go now! I recollect when you were the gayest dressed of any in the house.' To which Smith tells us Nollekens replied, 'That is more than I could ever say of you.'

Boswell, we are told, seldom washed himself, so that when he was well dressed his clean ruffles showed up the griminess of his skin. He was by no means the only gentleman of the eighteenth century about whom the same could be said.

Round about 1780 clothes became simpler and more natural. Although many people lived rather artificial lives, they were also, especially in England, interested in nature and country life and sport. Even in France the Queen, Marie Antoinette, and her ladies sometimes pretended to be shepherdesses and milkmaids. English people had always been enthusiastic about country sports such as hunting, and during the seventeenth and eighteenth centuries a great many well-to-do men built or rebuilt fine new country-houses for themselves. So plenty of people were ready to be influenced by writers and poets who wrote about nature and simple living.

Some of the first people to benefit by the new ideas were the children. Perhaps you have noticed that we have had very little to say about children's clothes. The reason is that for centuries children had been dressed exactly as their parents were—not like children at all but like miniature men and women. In Ancient Egypt, Greece and Rome, young children often wore no clothes at all, and if they did wear tunics and cloaks like those worn by their parents it did not matter, as they were loose and did not interfere with the child's freedom to grow and move about and play.

But from the fifteenth century onwards, as we have seen, men and women wore clothes that were often very peculiar indeed—tight, thick, heavy and often extremely uncomfortable. But it does not seem to have occurred to anyone that the clothes in which they chose to dress themselves were not equally suitable for their little girls and boys. So generations of children, particularly if the parents belonged to the upper classes, must have suffered great misery in their stiff, stuffed garments, their ruffs and whisks, their heavy brocades and their cloth of gold, or their silks and satins which so easily got dirty. Old pictures show us quite tiny babies in their nurses' or mothers' arms, dressed in the heavy fabrics and stiff styles worn by their parents.

In the eighteenth century little girls were put into tight corsets and wore hoops or panniers, tight bodices and powdered hair just as their mothers did. Little boys, too, wore satin and velvet breeches, embroidered coats and waistcoats, and had their hair curled, pomaded and powdered until they looked just like their fathers. Like small boys in earlier centuries, they were even fitted out with miniature swords.

Such clothes must have been very difficult to play in, and the children of wealthy people must often have envied the children of the poor, who could not afford fashionable clothes for their children or for themselves.

In the last half of the eighteenth century a French writer

named Jean-Jacques Rousseau wrote books in which he urged that people should be free and equal, and that children should be allowed to be children and not be treated as miniature adults. Some of Rousseau's ideas may have helped to cause the French Revolution, but those concerning children did nothing but good. Between 1770 and 1780, first of all in England, people began for the first time to dress their children in comfortable clothes which were quite different from those worn by their mothers and fathers. Little girls were freed from corsets, hoops and heavy petticoats and were dressed in simple (though still long) frocks with a sash round the waist; little boys were dressed in

Late eighteenth century children

long trousers, or 'pantaloons' as they were called (their fathers still wore knee breeches), short jackets without tails, similar to those which sailors wore at that time, and open-necked shirts. Both boys and girls were freed from wigs, hair powder and elaborate hair-dressing, and both wore flat-heeled shoes.

The new ideas about children's clothes gradually spread so

that by 1785 even the children of the French nobility were wearing 'English dress' as they called it. One French baron has described how until he was ten or eleven years old he wore satin coats and breeches and a small sword, and his hair was pomaded, powdered and arranged in rows of curls. Then his father decided that his children should wear the simpler clothes which some of his friends' children were already wearing, and his son tells of the joy with which he discarded his silks and satins, curls and powder, and put on the clothes which he calls the 'dress of English sailors'.

We can see portraits of little boys and girls dressed in these simpler clothes in many picture galleries. They were painted by such artists as Reynolds, Gainsborough and Romney.

After about 1780 the fashions worn by grown-up people, especially women, changed a great deal. Women stopped wearing their hair high above their heads, and instead they puffed it out on each side to make their heads look wide. They gave up hoops and side-panniers, and if they wore any kind of bustle under their dresses, it was at the back. They often turned back their overskirts and looped and draped them in festoons over the petticoat.

Men wore small perukes, if they wore any at all, but more and more men were wearing their own long hair, and, of course, pomading and powdering it. This disturbed the peruke-makers very much, and they even presented a petition to the king on the subject. All the same, some peruke-makers themselves wore their own hair, and this annoyed people so much that sometimes mobs attacked such men and cut their hair off. If the peruke-makers wanted other men to wear perukes, the mob saw no reason why they should not be compelled to wear them themselves.

The eighteenth century was a period of delicate colours, dainty patterns and soft materials. Elegant ladies and gentlemen, although they wore silk, satin, fine linen, and, when they could afford it, gold and silver brocade, also wore cotton fabrics printed with charming patterns. At first these printed cottons were imported from India. In France the wearing of them was forbidden because the authorities were afraid they would compete with the French silk industry, and when the laws were ignored they were made more severe. Dealers who brought printed cottons into the country and sold them could be hanged, whilst women wearing dresses made of printed cottons could

An eighteenth century looped skirt

have them torn off in public by the toll collector. But in spite of all this, people went on using the forbidden material for dresses and furnishing, and smugglers did a roaring trade.

Traders brought Indian cottons to London, as well as spices from the east and silks from China. But after the new world across the Atlantic had been discovered, and people from Europe had settled there, raw American cotton began to reach

England. English people spun it and wove it into fabrics, chiefly in Lancashire because the damp climate was especially suitable.

At first the fabrics were usually made with a linen warp and a cotton weft, as at that time men did not know how to make the cotton thread strong enough for the warp. Merchants supplied the warp to the weavers' own homes, which were usually in country districts. The weavers had to buy the raw cotton for themselves, and it was then picked over and cleaned by their children and spun into thread by their wives and daughters. But a good weaver could weave as much thread as several women could spin, so that he would often have to trudge from cottage to cottage to buy more thread, or would have to stop work while more thread was spun.

In the middle of the eighteenth century all this began to change. First a weaver named Hargreaves invented the 'spinning jenny' as it came to be called, which spun several threads at once instead of only one as the spinning-wheel had done. He was no more popular than the Rev. Wm. Lee had been when he invented the stocking frame. Spinners broke into his house and smashed his machine because they thought it would rob them of their way of making a living. Nevertheless, his spinning-jenny was used, and later the 'spinning-mule' which was an improvement thought out by a man named Crompton. The mule was worked by water-power, so that buildings to hold the machine had to be built by running streams, just as flour mills and fulling mills were.

The threads made by the spinning-jenny and the spinning-mule were still only suitable for weft threads. Then a man named Arkwright invented a machine that could spin threads strong enough to be used for the warp. He opened a factory at Cromford in Derbyshire, where his machines were worked by water-power, and was partner in a number of other factories. Meanwhile a Dr. Cartwright had invented a machine that speeded up the weaving of the large quantities of thread that could now be produced. Cotton fabrics became cheaper and easier to get than they had ever been before.

But, unfortunately, the cotton trade was for a long time linked up with a very terrible one—the slave trade. Merchants from Liverpool took Lancashire cotton goods to Africa, where they exchanged them for negro slaves. They then took the slaves across the Atlantic to America for sale, and returned to England laden with raw cotton, tobacco and sugar.

In Britain cotton as well as woollen fabrics were now carried from place to place loaded on the backs of horses or mules, or packed into lumbering wagons with wide wheels and drawn by six or eight horses over roads that were often a foot or more deep in mud.

Boots and shoes, too, were made by workers in their own homes from leather they collected from the merchants. The old stitchmen, as they were called, could make a boot from beginning to end by hand, and when the boots were ready they returned them to the merchants and were paid by him. The merchant sent boots and shoes to London or other big towns in baskets loaded on to the slow wagons of the time, and himself followed later on horseback or by fast coach. He and his customers, the shopkeepers, would meet probably in a tavern to do their business. The merchant would have shoes to sell, and also knee-length boots, as well as short boots. They were all, of course, of leather, not of rubber, as our wellingtons are to-day.

An eighteenth century high-heeled shoe

CHAPTER 20

France Imitates Ancient Greece

We all know how, during the French Revolution, many of the aristocrats of France were driven to execution through the streets of Paris, and how most of them went proudly past the howling mobs, elegantly dressed and dignified to the last.

The French Revolution filled men's minds, not only in France, but in neighbouring countries, and it led to many changes in the way European people lived and thought and, of course, in the way they dressed.

Even before the Revolution, as we have seen, fashionable dress was becoming simpler, except at court functions and on other special occasions. Men were more inclined to wear plain woollen fabrics and women simple printed cottons, and both men and women were dressing their hair more naturally. Huge hoops and panniers were being discarded, and children's clothes were simple and comfortable.

But after the Revolution something happened in France that had never happened before in the history of clothes—people deliberately copied the dress of a past age and country. France had become a republic, and French people were keenly interested in the republic of Ancient Greece that had flourished two thousand years before. They tried to imitate the Greeks, and to dress like them—or rather, the women did.

It is true that the imitation was not a very exact one. But the change from the clothes of a few years before was amazing. French women discarded their corsets and petticoats and appeared in long, straight, high-waisted dresses with short sleeves, worn over pink silk tights. The dresses were made of thin muslin or gauze or some similar fabric, and were often very like those which had been worn by little girls for some years—except that the adult dresses were often very long, with sometimes a train at the back. Some of them, even, were made like straight tunics and had draw strings round the neck and below the breast to draw them up to the size required.

Sometimes an over-tunic of a thin material was worn over

After the French Revolution

these simple dresses, and quite often a little jacket of a darker, thicker material was worn even indoors. In winter it might be fur-lined and buttoned up to the throat.

With their new style of dress women often wore flat sandals, with ribbons criss-crossed up their legs, over flesh-coloured stockings, or none. Their hair was sometimes cut short and curled. When it was long it was arranged in a knot at the back, with little curls on the forehead. Out of doors women often wore a kind of bonnet with a wide brim which we call a poke-bonnet.

Naturally these clothes, so utterly different from those of a few years before, scandalized many people. But they were imitated everywhere, all the same, and from the 1790s until about 1820 dresses of the kind worn by French women were the fashion in neighbouring countries as well, and in America. But in most countries, including France, most women seem to have worn at least one petticoat under the flimsy dresses. But unnecessary petticoats, corsets and high-heeled shoes were discarded everywhere, except by old-fashioned people. Wide skirts and hoops survived only, sometimes, at court. In England they were not abolished at court until 1820, when George IV came to the throne.

FRANCE IMITATES ANCIENT GREECE

In the 1790s silk became very expensive. The best silks had been produced in France, and France at this time was too busy attending to other matters to give much time to silk weaving. A little silk was woven in England, but not very much, and during this time, fine, thin and often very lovely cotton materials became even more popular than before, and continued to be worn even after silk could be bought again easily.

Another French industry that was almost destroyed by the Revolution was that of lace-making. Thirty factories closed, and many of the lace-makers emigrated, chiefly to Belgium. After Napoleon became Emperor of France he tried to revive the use of lace, for the sake of the lace industry. Court dress in France became more formal again. Velvet and satin were used (though not hoops or full skirts) and gentlemen were required to wear lace frills at their wrists and lace ends to their cravats. Ladies sometimes wore court dresses made entirely of lace. But the old enthusiasm for it was dead.

With their short-sleeved dresses women wore long gloves, and carried hand-bags to take the place of the pockets which before they had worn tied round their waists under their full skirts, or hanging from their belts. In the winter they sometimes carried very large muffs and in the summer tiny parasols.

Frenchmen, in spite of their interest in Greek life and thought, did not attempt to revive the Greek way of dressing. They continued to wear coats that were short in front with long skirts or tails at the back, short waistcoats and knee-breeches. The cuffs and ruffles of earlier days disappeared for ordinary everyday dress, and their clothes, on the whole, became very

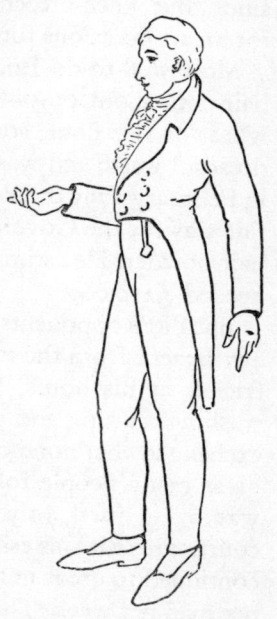

Man's suit after the French Revolution

221

plain. The only decorations were a velvet collar, metal or pearl buttons, small frills, perhaps, at the wrist and throat, and sometimes a fancy waistcoat. In some ways their clothes became less comfortable than they had been before, as they took to wearing very high collars on their coats and to wrapping big white neck cloths or cravats round their necks, tying them in front with a bow After about 1800 the cravat, which might be black or white, was usually fastened at the back, without a bow.

In the 1790s some men began to wear pantaloons, which, like the knee-breeches, were very tight. They reached to the calf, and were very like the pantaloons small boys had begun to wear twenty years or so earlier. As time went on the pantaloons were made full-length, and then they gradually began to get a little looser and more like the trousers that men have worn ever since. But knee-breeches and white silk stockings were worn for smart occasions for a long time.

Most well-to-do English people continued to powder their hair until about 1795—although, as the powder was made from wheat or rice flour, some were beginning to feel that it was a dreadful waste and was helping to keep bread expensive. Then in February 1795 the Prime Minister, William Pitt, thought of a fine way for the Government to raise money. He decided to tax hair powder. He estimated that the tax would bring in a much-needed £210,000.

But Pitt's opponents were determined that he should not reap any benefit from the tax. The Duke of Beaufort assembled his friends at his home, Woburn Abbey, and there was a great washing, cutting and combing of hair, and solemn vows were exchanged that none of them would use hair powder again. A great many people followed their example, and soon powder was being used only by elderly or old-fashioned people, at court, where it was essential until 1820, and by the army, which continued to use it until 1799 at the rate of one pound of flour per man per week. The people who went on using hair-powder paid a guinea a year for the privilege, and were therefore, of course, called guinea pigs. It is rather surprising to find that when the Act was repealed in 1869 the tax was still being paid by about eight hundred people.

The three-cornered cocked hat went right out of fashion, and the hat turned up back and front which we associate with Napoleon was worn by a great many men. It was part of court costume and was worn with some uniforms for a long time, but after about 1800 the top hat became the most popular kind of head gear, and it remained fashionable for the whole of the

Hats of Napoleon's time

nineteenth century, and is still worn for formal occasions to-day.

Because men's clothes became plainer it does not mean that men took less interest in them. The 'beaux', as the elegantly dressed gentlemen of the time were called, insisted on the most perfect fit for their coats and skin-tight breeches, and spent hours tying and arranging their cravats. They still very often wore corsets to pinch in their waists and help to make their clothes set well. They carried canes, which were sometimes hollow and concealed a sword, since the wearing of swords was no longer fashionable, and they peered at the world through 'quizzing glasses'—which were magnifying glasses on a handle. They wore gloves in delicate colours, but not embroidered or decorated very much. Napoleon himself seems to have been as keen on gloves as some previous emperors. He is said to have had two hundred and thirty pairs of cream-coloured gloves, and forty-two with fur linings.

So far as fashions for women were concerned, Paris led the way, but during the French Revolution and afterwards, London became leader in all matters concerned with men's clothing.

From about the year 1800 until 1812 the 'dictator' of fashion, for men, was a man named George Bryan Brummell—Beau Brummell, as he is generally called. Brummell did not introduce any new or outlandish styles—in fact he taught that to be really well-dressed a man must not be conspicuous. He should be outstanding only because of the perfect fit of his clothes, his 'grooming' and his absolute cleanliness. 'No scents, but plenty of clean linen' was one of Brummell's slogans. His insistence on cleanliness, not only of linen but of the people who wore it, must have made fashionable life much pleasanter.

Brummell's influence was so great that men all over Europe adopted his ideas, and the Prince Regent, who later became George IV, is said to have wept when Beau Brummell did not approve of the set of his coat. Brummell himself would not emerge from his room until his slightly starched cravat was perfectly arranged, and if that did not happen at the first attempt he discarded the cravat and tried another. There is a famous story about his valet emerging from his master's room with a basket full of slightly crumpled cravats which he explained were 'our failures'.

Brummell quarrelled with the Prince Regent, and he spent his last years in France, living in poverty. But his views on the kind of clothes well-dressed men should wear have influenced male dress ever since.

For centuries men's clothes had been just as fantastic and extravagant in every way as those of women—and in some periods a great deal more so. No fabric, colour or decoration was worn by women that was not also worn by men. But now all this was changing. For the first time silks and satins, lace and ribbons, feathers, jewels and delicate colours were considered unmanly. From this time—the end of the eighteenth century—onwards men's clothes became steadily more and more sombre, and 'fashion' became a subject in which only women were supposed to be interested.

It seems odd that it was at this time, when men's clothes were thicker and gave them more protection than before, that a bold character named Jonas Hanway began to dare ridicule by carrying an umbrella. Ever since the early days of the eighteenth

Pantalettes

century umbrellas—heavy, clumsy things, sometimes of leather —had been known, and parasols, of course, for protecting ladies' complexions from the glare of the sun had been used in many countries for centuries. But Hanway, with his umbrella, was considered very effeminate, and few people followed his example. The umbrellas of his time were still clumsy and awkward, and it was not until the middle of the nineteenth century that, with steel frames, they became lighter. By that time it was no longer considered peculiar for either men or women to be seen carrying them.

Children were dressed after the French Revolution very much as they had been before, boys in short jackets and pantaloons, girls in low-necked, puff-sleeved frocks, with sashes round their waists. Their frocks were now very much like those worn by their mothers. Tiny boys were dressed exactly like their sisters, but during Napoleon's time they began to wear 'pantalettes'— ankle-length trousers or drawers made of white cotton or linen —under their short dresses.

Women and little girls, after a time, also wore pantalettes with frills at the ankles, which were meant to show below their long frocks. But women soon gave them up, though little girls went on wearing them for a long time.

CHAPTER 21

The Age of the Crinoline

One would have thought that once women had escaped from tight corsets and full, heavy skirts they would refuse ever to be imprisoned in them again. But that was not the case.

After a few years the straight, narrow-looking dresses began to widen out at the hem in a bell-shape, with one or two starched petticoats under them to hold them out. Then the high waist dropped to its natural position, skirts became wider still, and sleeves became very wide and full at the shoulders—so that women looked rather the shape of an hour-glass or a letter X. It became tremendously important to have a very small, narrow waist. By about 1825 the very women who, in their own youth, had worn loose, comfortable dresses, were helping their daughters to squeeze themselves into the tightest possible corsets.

There are a great many early nineteenth-century cartoons showing daughters gripping bed-posts while their mothers, and sometimes their fathers as well, tug at the laces of their corsets to get them tight. Fashion books of the time advise mothers to get their daughters to lie face downwards on the floor so that the mother can put her foot in the small of the daughter's back and so get a good grip on the laces.

For a time, with the bell-shaped skirts, women gave up dressing their hair simply, and instead they piled it up on the tops of their heads again in curls and loops, and decorated it with flowers, feathers and bows. When they went out they wore large bonnets, also covered with plumes and flowers. But by about 1840 this style had died out and most women parted their hair in the centre and dressed it very smoothly and plainly. Often they wore caps indoors and small bonnets out of doors.

By this time they were again wearing tight, smooth bodices, often with a point at the waist in front again. And the skirts became wider and wider with, under them, as many as six or

An early nineteenth century bell-shaped dress

An 'hour-glass' dress

eight petticoats, one or two, perhaps, being of red flannel. The outer, cotton, one was stiffly starched and decorated with frills and lace. Sometimes one of the petticoats would be made of a stiff material called crinoline, of which the warp was of horsehair and the weft of wool. Or a quilted petticoat might be worn. It is strange to think that, although the climate had not changed, women in 1800 were wearing one thin dress and only one petticoat, while their grand-daughters in 1850 used as many as forty-eight yards of fabric to make one frock, and wore under it as many as seven petticoats. A skirt had to measure at least ten yards round the hem, and might measure as much as twenty or twenty-five yards.

Full skirt—nineteenth century

Unfortunately the change in fashion was not confined to grown-up people. Children who, you remember, had been simply and sensibly dressed at the beginning of the century, were, as time went on, again dressed very much as their elders were. Girls suffered more than boys. The only thing to be said in favour of their clothes towards the middle of the nineteenth century is that they gradually became shorter than they had ever been before—though the long pantalettes to the ankle were still worn by little girls. But the skirts, like those of their mothers, became wider and wider, with frills and flounces, braid and ribbon trimmings, and under them a large number of petticoats.

Boys' clothes did not change so much, except that their long trousers became tighter. But, unfortunately for them, they

Victorian children

were not put into boys' clothes until they were quite big, and in French and English fashion plates in which children appear it is quite difficult to tell which of the children are boys and which are girls. Both wore full skirts, frilly petticoats, ribbon and feather-trimmed hats, sometimes boots made of silk, and, if they were out of doors, kid gloves. The only differences between them were that the little boys usually had slightly shorter hair, and, after girls stopped wearing pantalettes, little boys were still put into a rather short pantalette which showed for a few inches below their frocks.

Men's clothes did not change so much as women's did, ex-

THE AGE OF THE CRINOLINE

cept that they tended to become darker and gloomier. Until about 1830 well-dressed men might wear light or fancy waistcoats and bright buttons with their cut-away coats, but after that the waistcoat, like the coat, was often of black cloth, and the coat was more likely to be a frock coat, with spreading skirts and a tight waist. The long trousers were often rather tight and were strapped down under the foot. Top hats were worn by nearly every townsman, also side whiskers and beards.

Even the first policemen wore top hats, with their swallow-tailed coats and, in summer, white trousers. Lamp lighters, and other working men, wore them, too, and such people as telegraph workers climbed up ladders and telegraph poles with top hats on their heads, inside which, we are told, they carried their small tools. We often read of men shopping and carrying the small purchases home on the tops of their heads inside their hats.

But, of course, men's clothes varied according to the position of the wearer, and the purpose for which the clothes were being worn. Doctors, ministers, and other professional men wore black frock-coats and top hats nearly always. Certain other men might wear them only for attending church, for weddings and funerals and for 'best' wear generally, while for ordinary everyday wear they might wear striped or checked trousers and short coats, or, if they were countrymen, knee breeches and gaiters.

The real country worker, in England, wore until the end of the nineteenth century a garment that was probably descended from the tunics that his ancestors had worn centuries before. It was called a smock—which is a very old English word. Women's under-tunics, or chemises, were called smocks in Saxon times. The countryman's smock of the eighteenth and nineteenth centuries was made of very strong, stiff linen, black for weekdays and white for Sundays. It was rather a full garment, and was drawn in across the back and chest and at the wrists with beautiful and often very elaborate honeycomb stitchery, which is still called 'smocking' because it was used on the countryman's smock.

A garment similar to the Englishman's smock but without the honeycomb stitchery is still worn by French porters and other working men. It is generally blue. And all over Europe there are districts where country people still wear peasant costumes in a style and colour that have come down to them from centuries ago. Often they are embroidered, or the fabrics

A countryman in a smock

are woven into certain patterns that are distinctive of the particular place. Sometimes the head-dresses, especially those worn by the women, are very striking indeed, and may vary from village to village in one area.

Many machines, besides those for spinning and weaving, were invented or developed during the eighteenth and nineteenth centuries and took work out of people's homes and into factories. We have seen how, in Queen Elizabeth I's reign, a stocking-knitting machine had been invented and had not been very popular with the hand-knitters. But in time such a machine, worked, like spinning wheels, by the hands and feet of the workers in their own homes, had come into use. But in the eighteenth century stocking machines had been invented that could be worked by power and which knitted several stockings at once. When they were first introduced there were riots and bloodshed in many places, for the unfortunate stocking-makers were terrified that their livelihood was to be taken away from them. They declared, too, that the machines made inferior stockings. For some time bands of wreckers, working very secretly and at dead of night, attacked the new factories, first in one place and then in another, and smashed the machines. The men were usually called Luddites, because their leader was supposed to be a man named Ned Ludd who, like Robin Hood, had his headquarters in the depths of Sherwood Forest.

Of course, the machines won in the end, and stocking-makers, like spinners and weavers, had to work in the factories and live near their work.

Gradually steam power took the place of the water power which had been used at first, and the new factories were built within easy reach of the coal mines. So the country people who had supported themselves by doing all kinds of things in their own homes had to move to the new towns that sprang up near the factories. Places such as Manchester, which had been little villages, soon became large and important towns.

Another thing that was made by machine in factories for the first time during the nineteenth century was lace. Also for the first time, cotton thread was used instead of linen for making it. Hand-made lace continued to be made (and still is) in many places in England, France, Belgium, Italy and other countries, but machine-made lace was so much cheaper that only a few could afford to buy hand-made lace. Queen Victoria had a bridal gown of lace made at Honiton in Devon, and the Empress Eugénie of France also tried to revive its use. But although lace became popular again in the nineteenth century, it was machine-made lace that was generally used.

Machines for carrying out the various processes connected with boot-making were also invented during the nineteenth century and caused great indignation and bitterness. There were strikes, and bootmakers, like stocking-knitters, threatened to smash the machines which they thought were going to rob them of their livelihood.

Boots and shoes, until towards the end of the nineteenth century, were made straight, so that they could be worn on either foot, and people were careful to change them from foot to foot each day so that they would wear evenly. Sometimes we read that the soldiers who were fighting in the Crimean war were sent (through somebody's carelessness) supplies of boots which were all for the left foot. But this, of course, was impossible at that time, as all army boots were 'straights', and boots in pairs, one for the left and one for the right foot, were not supplied until some time later.

Country people and the factory workers in the new towns nearly all wore clogs with wooden soles and leather uppers. During the summer the cloggers lived in rough shelters, or tents, in the forests. They had a low bench inside the shelter, to which a big knife was attached at one end by a hook in such a way that it could be swung round in different directions. It had a long handle at the other end. The cloggers cut their blocks of alder, birch or sycamore with a few strokes of the knife into roughly the shape of a shoe sole, and hollowed out the instep with another knife. Then with a third knife they made a groove to which the uppers would be attached. The rough soles were taken to the clogger's shop in the village or town to be finished.

Gloves were still, as a rule, sewn by hand by women in their own cottages (and a few still are) after they had been cut out in factories to the right size. Glove-makers usually possessed a 'glover's donkey', which was a kind of vice on a stand about three feet high, which the worker gripped between her knees. Her foot worked a lever which opened the vice for her to insert the two edges to be sewn, which were then gripped firmly. The brass edges of the vice were marked with regular grooves to guide the worker's needle in sewing.

As, during the nineteenth century, the clothes worn by women and girls gradually became more bulky and heavy, a few people protested and urged that the fashion should be changed. One of the best known of these people was an American lady named Mrs. Amelia Bloomer. She had started a paper called *The Lily* in 1840. Mrs. Bloomer felt very strongly that women should have a great deal more freedom than they had at that time, and in particular she urged them to get rid of their cumbersome and uncomfortable clothes. She designed an outfit for women which she thought was simple, comfortable and healthy. Drawings of it appeared in her paper, and she herself wore it.

Mrs. Bloomer's outfit consisted of a dress or tunic of figured silk with high neck and long sleeves. It reached to a few inches below the knee. Under it she wore a pair of trousers something like those worn by Turkish women, and made of the same material as the dress. On her head Mrs. Bloomer wore a straw hat with a four and a half-inch brim, lined with white silk. The hat was trimmed with a plain ribbon.

To us Mrs. Bloomer's outfit does not seem very outlandish or extraordinary. But it was a complete contrast to the fashionable clothes being worn at the time, so only a few 'advanced' women in America followed Mrs. Bloomer's example and wore it. In 1851, the year of the Great Exhibition in London for which the Crystal Palace was built,

The clothes worn by
Mrs. Bloomer

the new costume appeared in England, and the *Illustrated London News* had an article about it and pictures of it. On the whole, most papers spoke favourably of it, though others described it as 'indecent' and the trousers as 'masculine', and only a few brave women were courageous enough to wear it and face the ridicule it caused. It was not taken up by any society woman with a great deal of influence, but only by unimportant people who were not leaders of fashion. And, of course, it was abused by everyone connected with the dressmaking trade.

Deliberate attempts to change fashion have nearly always failed, and Mrs. Bloomer's efforts were no exception. Instead of simpler clothes being adopted, clothes, for women, developed during the next half century in quite a different direction.

It is a very curious fact that women's changing fashions have developed in very much the same way in three different centuries. In the sixteenth century skirts were bell shaped until about the middle of the century, when the Spanish farthingale, or hoop, was introduced to spread them out to a great width. This was followed by the French farthingale, which widened the dresses at the sides but not at the back and front. In the eighteenth century full gathered skirts led again to the adoption of the hoop to support them, which in turn was replaced by panniers to widen the dress at the hips while keeping it narrow from front to back. In the nineteenth century something rather similar happened. By the 1850s women were so loaded with heavy skirts and petticoats that something had to be done. The problem was solved, not by abandoning the full skirts, but by again introducing a steel hoop for women to wear under their dresses to support them. The hoops were quite light—only about half a pound in weight which was much less than the weight of six or seven petticoats—and the result was that the dresses, or crinolines as we call the hooped skirts, became still wider, in fact, really enormous.

At this time women, like men, often wore dark coloured, or black, materials, and their dresses, except for evening wear, were high at the throat with long sleeves (often very wide at the wrist) and were trimmed with braid, fringe, or strips of velvet. They wore jet ornaments, or cameos, or heavy gold lockets and brooches.

Photography had been invented by this time, so for the first time we are able to see pictures of people in the clothes of a past age exactly as they were and not through the eyes of an artist. The men and women of mid-Victorian photographs always look rather solemn, and the clothes make even the young look rather elderly.

Over their crinolines women wore straight, short coats, or capes, or even more often shawls, when they went out, and on their heads they wore small hats or bonnets tied under their chins with wide ribbons. No lady ever thought of going out without a hat and gloves, and a great many wore gloves or mittens indoors, even at meal-times or when playing cards or musical instruments. We read of little girls being made to wear gloves when sewing or doing embroidery, just as many of their elders did. Many ladies considered it rather indecent to appear anywhere without gloves, and we read of at least one elderly lady who boasted that in all her life no gentleman had ever touched her bare hand. For although men removed their glove to shake hands, it was not, of course, correct for women to do so then, any more than it is now.

About 1860 a machine was invented that was to be a great blessing, and was to save tailors and dressmakers, as well as mothers of families, many hours of drudgery. It was the sewing machine and, unlike most machines, it came into people's own homes. Until that time every stitch of the elaborate clothes that both men and women had worn for centuries had been done by hand, and hours and hours of patient work had been needed in order to make even the simplest gown or coat or petticoat. The sewing machine gradually changed all that—though its first effect was not altogether good. Dressmakers were so thrilled to discover how much they could do in a short time that they plunged into an orgy of frilling, pleating, puffing, ruching and tucking. And the huge, over-decorated skirts were placed over larger and larger hoops.

Women who worked in factories and shops wore the hooped-skirt just as women of the wealthy classes and of the nobility did. In 1863 a pottery firm in Staffordshire reported that two hundred pounds' worth of pottery had been swept to the ground and smashed in one year by the crinolines of the women who worked for them.

Nineteenth century lady wearing crinoline and shawl

Though the crinoline had its disadvantages, it had one great advantage. The huge skirt made almost any waist look small, so there was not quite so much tight lacing.

After about 1869 the crinoline was gradually flattened in front and the fulness of the skirt was drawn to the back. Then the crinoline was given up altogether, and something happened

THE AGE OF THE CRINOLINE

rather similar to what we have seen happening in earlier centuries. The full upper skirts were drawn up over the underskirt and formed into loops at the sides and back. Then women began to wear 'bustles'—cage-like supports of steel wire and horsehair which they tied round their waists and which held up great piles of drapery at the back.

For a short time, in the late 1870s, the bustle disappeared and women wore dresses that were tight fitting to the knees, and draped and pleated from there to the ground. But before long the bustle returned and was worn until about 1890.

Unfortunately, with the disappearance of the crinoline tight lacing returned, in spite of the protests of doctors and other thoughtful people. No woman was considered beautiful or stylish unless she had a tiny waist, so quite young girls were put into tight corsets so that their waists could not develop. A Victorian magazine tells us of a girls' boarding school where the girls were sealed into their stays by the head mistress. The stays were only removed for one hour on Saturdays so that the girls could wash themselves. By this means the waist of a fifteen-year-old girl which meas-

Late nineteenth century dress with a bustle

ured twenty-three inches could be reduced to thirteen inches in two years, we are told.

No wonder many girls were delicate, and went into declines and died young.

239

At the same time, boys' coats became tighter, and their necks were forced into hard Eton collars instead of the soft collars they had been wearing for some years.

But although some little girls were tightly corseted and were dressed in frilled and flounced frocks over crinolines and bustles, there were, of course, many others whose parents still dressed their children more simply, in clothes such as those we see in pictures of Alice in Wonderland. Nearly all children, boys and girls, wore a pinafore at home and at play, as Alice does. It might be white and trimmed with frills and lace, or it might be of checked or black material and quite plain.

Clothes worn by Alice in Wonderland

As time went on even the fashionable child's clothes began to get simpler. Boys were still kept in petticoats until they were about six years old, but after that their parents began to put them into short breeches and blouses with sailor collars. But they were soon old enough for long trousers and stiff collars. So far as little girls were concerned, an artist named Kate Greenaway had a great deal of influence. In her charming drawings she showed children dressed in clothes something like those that children had worn a hundred years before—girls in loose high-waisted frocks with sashes and short sleeves and boys in pantaloons and open-necked shirts—and some parents in the eighties began to dress their children, especially the little girls, in similar clothes.

By the end of the nineteenth century children, even in fashionable circles, were no longer dressed like miniature adults. Many little girls wore sailor blouses, as their small brothers did, with kilted skirts. They were blue or white and of woollen cloth for winter and linen or cotton for summer. Party frocks were, of course, more frilly, but were still simple, and little

THE AGE OF THE CRINOLINE

girls were no longer put into tight corsets. Their dresses still came below their knees, and gradually lengthened as they got older, until they put their hair up when they were about eighteen and their skirts, like those of their mothers, touched the ground, or even had a train at the back.

In the 1870s the bicycle was invented, and first men and then women began to cycle about the country. People also began to play more games than they had done in the past, and even women played tennis and golf, as well as croquet which, before that, had been almost their only outdoor game.

A little girl in a
sailor suit

For these outdoor activities they had to wear slightly shorter skirts—though they were still very long according to our standards, since they were never shorter than ankle length.

But even after women gave up wearing the bustle they still wore tight corsets to keep their waists small, and for ordinary wear their dresses trailed on the ground or even had trains. Many women began to wear separate blouses and skirts, and often, with plain blouses, they imitated men by wearing stiff collars and ties. But the blouses or bodices could be very frilly, and the sleeves in the nineties were always enormous, like balloons, at the shoulders, and tight lower down. All dresses had high collars, usually right up under the chin.

But for cycling the really advanced girl wore a shirt blouse with a divided 'skirt'—called 'bloomers' after the lady who had tried to introduce simpler clothes in the 1840s and 1850s. The bloomers of the nineties were not really a bit like the soft, thin, silk trousers, gathered at the ankle, which Mrs. Bloomer had worn. The cycling bloomers were of tweed or some other stout cloth, were very full, and reached to a few inches above the ankle. With them the lady cyclist wore boots.

Q   241

The cycling outfit caused a great uproar and was strongly disapproved of. Many women would not think of wearing it, and cycled in their long, full, thick skirts, just as they walked, played tennis, and even climbed mountains in them.

Late nineteenth century lady   Woman in cycling outfit

Men, for sports such as cycling, walking and fishing, returned to knee-breeches, or knickerbockers, as they were now often called, and wore them with belted coats called Norfolk jackets, and caps, all probably of tweed. Although men still wore top hats and frock coats for all formal occasions, a wide variety of other hats and caps were now worn, including round hard straw hats with flat brims. Women wore these hard uncomfortable hats—boaters as they were often called—as well.

CHAPTER 22

What Will Come Next ?

At the beginning of the century we are living in now several things were happening that were to lead, in time, to changes in the way people lived and, therefore, dressed. We have already mentioned cycling, and the greater interest people were taking in games. At school girls were now doing gymnastics and were playing such games as hockey, netball, lacrosse and tennis. Many of them continued to play games after they left school. Grown-up players, for some time, went on wearing long skirts and high-necked blouses but they began to dislike very much the idea of being tightly laced into heavy, stiff corsets. Rubber and elastic were used more and more, and corsets became lighter and more comfortable. Schoolgirls were no longer as a rule put into corsets at all. Gym tunics, or skirts worn over a dark blouse in winter and a white one in summer, became almost a school uniform for girls.

Schoolboys (unless they were at the kind of school where they had to wear Eton suits and top hats) usually wore cloth breeches which buttoned below the knee, and either Norfolk jackets or straight short jackets similar to those worn to-day. But they all wore stiff, starched collars. The school hats of both boys and girls were often hard straw boaters, though boys sometimes wore caps. Girls tied their long hair back with a big bow of black ribbon. Or they might have one or two plaits. They nearly always wore long black stockings.

Women dressed their hair over pads to make it high or wide and they usually had a twist or bun on the tops of their heads. Their hats, which were usually very big and were trimmed with feathers or flowers did not fit down over their heads but were perched up

Q*

243

rather high and held on with long hatpins with fancy knobs at the ends. Often a spotted net veil was tied round the brim of the hat and drawn down tightly under the chin.

Another thing that was gradually altering people's lives was the motor-car. The earliest motor-cars were high, open vehicles which look very odd to us now when we see them taking part in a veteran car rally. When women rode in them they usually

A boy in a Norfolk suit

tied their big hats on with a wide gauze scarf which they put right over the hat and sometimes over their faces too. And they wore grey or fawn dust cloaks to protect their clothes from the dust which rose in clouds from the untarred roads.

By this time a great many women were wearing fitted suits, or costumes, which were made, like men's suits, by a tailor. The skirts almost or quite touched the ground, and at first they fitted closely over the hips and were generally pleated or flared in such a way that they were fairly wide at the hem. Frilled petticoats were worn under them and ladies had to learn how to lift their dresses gracefully when they were walking out of doors, or going up and down steps.

But after about 1908 there was a change. Skirts became shorter—about ankle length—and narrower, and about 1911 a terrible garment became fashionable which was called a hobble skirt. It was very straight and narrow all the way down, and not more than a yard round at the hem, so that women could

A motoring hat

take only short steps. It was very uncomfortable and even dangerous to wear, and, of course, it was laughed at, but it remained fashionable for a few years, though about 1912 it was often split up in front or at the sides to make walking a little easier.

With these scanty dresses petticoats, if they were worn at all, had to be very straight and slim, so starched and frilled cotton and linen petticoats, which had been part of every woman's wardrobe for so long, disappeared for a time.

WHAT WILL COME NEXT?

In 1914 came the First World War. Thousands of men and a great many women found themselves in uniform, and those who were not had many other things to think about than clothes. Women spent a lot of their time knitting warm sweaters, scarves, gloves and so forth for soldiers and sailors, and many of them knitted jumpers and sports coats for themselves for the first time. The knitted jumper and skirt fashion is one that has lasted ever since.

Hobble skirt

One result of the war was that people were less formal in their dress than they had been before. Fewer men wore tail coats and top hats, and a great many gave up wearing stiff collars for everyday wear and wore soft collars made of the same material as their shirts instead.

Girls might occasionally be seen out of doors or in public places without hats and gloves, though this habit was often frowned on by older women.

For a few years after the war women wore very plain dresses which they often made themselves. Although they probably did not know it, these dresses were almost exactly like the tunics

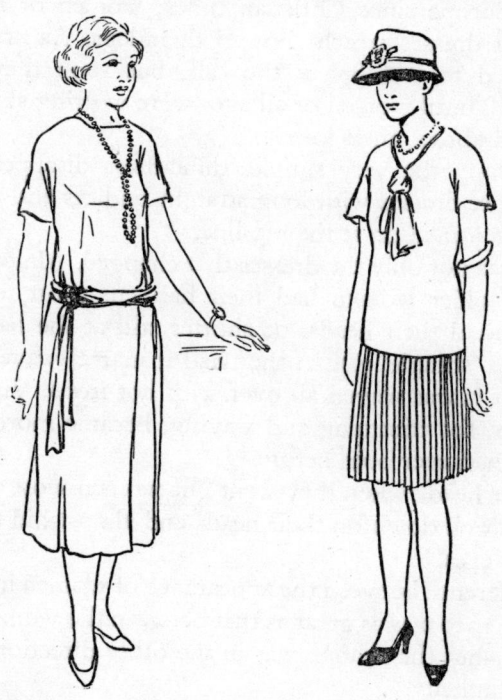

T-shaped dress worn after the first Great War

The long bodice and short skirt of the 1920s

which their ancestors wore hundreds and even thousands of years before. Scores of women now living can remember taking a strip of material, folding it across the centre, cutting out a round or V-shaped opening for the neck and two strips from the sides to make the garment T-shaped. Then, when they had machined up the side seams, turned up the hem and bound the neck and sleeves, they had a new dress which had taken them only an hour or so to make, and which only needed a belt to complete it.

But although these frocks were so very like the universal tunics of ancient times, there was one very big difference—something quite new. For the first time in the history of Western Europe since Christian times, women of all classes wore short dresses which showed their legs. At first dresses still reached to just below the calf, but soon they became shorter still, until women of all ages were wearing skirts about to, or even above, their knees.

Before long the very simple, tunic-dress disappeared, and women wore dresses with long straight bodices and with little short skirts joined on at the hip line.

But it was not only the dresses that changed. Almost all girls and many older women had their hair cut short, in a 'bob' straight round their heads, or shorter still at the back, like a man's, in a 'shingle'. Often they had it marcel waved—which means that it was waved all over with hot irons. Visits to the hairdresser, for trimming and waving, became more frequent than they had ever been before.

On their heads when they went out women wore small hats that fitted well down on their heads and almost hid their foreheads and eyes.

The difference between the appearance of women in 1900 and women in 1930 was as great as that between the women of 1800 and 1830—but the change was in the other direction, towards greater simplicity.

Evening dresses became long again after a time, and soon the shapes and lengths of day dresses began to change from year to year and became more complicated. But they have never returned, for ordinary wear, to the elaborate heavy clothes of the nineteenth century.

The simpler clothes which followed the First War made home dressmaking easier than it had been for several centuries. At the same time, however, something else was happening. Big factories were beginning to produce clothes for both men and

WHAT WILL COME NEXT?

women in large quantities and many sizes, so that people who in the past would have employed a tailor or dressmaker to make clothes especially for them, began to buy things ready-made. By the 1930s ready-made clothes, often from American factories, were very cheap, so that even quite poor people could buy them more easily and more frequently than ever before.

But in 1939 came the Second World War, and with it clothes rationing. For the first time people in England could not buy the clothes they wanted, even if they had the money, unless they also had enough coupons. Many people had to spend their time altering and repairing their old clothes and cutting them down for their children. Again many men and women spent years in uniform, and others made do with what they had. Clothes rationing continued for some years after the war, but once the shortages were over, clothes began to sell as never before.

There were several reasons for this. For one thing, young people were earning much more money than before the war. For the first time in history they had more to spend than their elders, and the designers and sellers of clothes quickly realized what this could mean. The chain stores began to sell clothes which were specially designed for young people; they were more varied, more interesting and of better quality than ready-made clothes had been before the war, and because they sold in such large quantities the prices were reasonably low.

The chain stores also began to employ young designers, who knew what other young people wanted and were not afraid to risk new and original styles. In fact, one of the tendencies of fashion in the 1960s has been to concentrate on clothes which were unusual and striking rather than obviously pretty. It seemed that many girls were more anxious to look startling than romantic, and some fashions seemed very surprising to older people; for instance, long black stockings, which had been regarded by schoolgirls in the 1930s as a particularly hideous feature of school uniform, became very fashionable.

Another new development of the 1960s was that young men became very much more interested in clothes and much more adventurous in their choice of what to wear. Ever since the

249

nineteenth century men's clothes had tended to be formal and correct, and anything unusual or noticeable was felt to be in bad taste. But now a much greater variety of colours and designs made their appearance. As with women's fashions, some of the styles seemed extravagant and even ugly to older people. The clothes of young men and young women became more alike than ever before; girls not only wore slacks (which had become common since the war) and jeans but took to trouser suits as well. But the more extravagant styles remained the preserve of the young, and the rest of the population continued to dress in a way that was not essentially very different from that of the 1920s and 1930s.

The way we dress is influenced by the materials we wear. For thousands of years men and women used silk, wool, cotton, linen and a few other fabrics, from which to make clothes. But in each case the fabric was woven from thread spun from substances produced by nature—by plants such as cotton and flax, or by living creatures such as silk worms and sheep.

But now scientists have learnt how to make fabrics in quite a different way. The first of the new fabrics was called, originally, artificial silk, but later that name was dropped and it was called rayon. It was made by dissolving wood pulp or some similar material in acid and then driving the thickish fluid through minute holes. The tiny streams that emerged were hardened by passing through air or through a bath of some suitable liquid, and became fine filaments, similar to the filament of silk which the silk worm produces. The rayon filaments were cut into short lengths and spun into threads which were then woven, either alone, or mixed with cotton, wool or silk, to make fabrics.

Rayon was used to make stockings—for when women started to wear short skirts they took far more interest in what their legs looked like than they had done before. Those who could afford it wore pure silk stockings, but for many women rayon took the place of the wool or cotton stockings which they had previously worn. Underclothes and dresses of all kinds were also made of rayon, of course.

WHAT WILL COME NEXT?

But rayon was only the first of the synthetic fabrics, and natural fibres from wood or plant forms were used in making it. Scientists went on experimenting until they could make synthetic threads from chemicals without the help first of all of any animal or vegetable material. They called the new fabric nylon. Incredibly fine threads of nylon could be produced, they found, which yet were very strong and tough.

Nylon was used during the war for all kinds of purposes, but it was not until the war had been over for some years that people could begin to buy it in the shops. Then it appeared in various forms and we found that the scientists, by using it in different ways and by blending it with other materials, could produce fabrics of many different kinds, from the finest possible gauze to the thickest imitation furs.

Experiments still went on, and after producing nylon scientists produced yet more new fabrics with special qualities, such as terylene—fabrics that dry quickly and need little or no ironing, or that do not crease, or that keep their pleats and creases even after washing, or that are windproof and warm, while at the same time being light.

New ways of making fabrics waterproof were discovered, too, so that it has become possible for us to buy thin, light garments that are cool to wear and yet keep us dry in wet weather. Waterproof nylon was much more attractive than earlier waterproof materials, and it was succeeded by the even smarter PVC (polyvinylchloride compound), which for the first time made rainwear positively fashionable.

Many of the trimmings we wear with our clothes—things such as hair combs and slides, buckles, buttons, the frames of handbags and so on—used to be made of tortoiseshell, or of horn or bone. Nowadays they are more often made of plastic materials—which means that a liquid made by scientists is poured into moulds of the right shape, and when it has hardened, which it does very quickly at the right temperature, the combs, or whatever it may be, are ready.

What effect are all these new materials going to have on the clothes of the future? Will all heavy, thick, bulky clothes in time disappear? Will a time come when there is *no* ironing or starching whatever? Will the fibres that have served man since the very beginnings of civilization—the wools and linens, cottons and silks—no longer be needed at all? And if so, what effect is that going to have on the lives of all the people all over the world who live by producing such fabrics?

Man will not know the answers to these questions for a very long time.

Neither can we imagine what shapes the garments of the future will take. Will men ever again wear light coloured, richly embroidered clothes like those of the eighteenth century? Or thickly padded ones like those of the sixteenth? Or will our descendants some day wear clothes similar to those the Ancient Greeks and Romans wore?

It does not seem very likely to us now that any of these things will happen, but the one thing certain about clothes is that they are constantly changing, sometimes suddenly, but more often so slowly that we hardly notice it. Each generation looks different from the one before and the one after it.

We can be quite certain that the clothes which seem natural and normal to us to-day will one day appear as old-fashioned and extraordinary to our descendants as those of the past seem to us.

Index

Aaron, 43, 44
Abraham, 42
Aegean civilization, 47, 51
Africa, 218
Alb, 91, 97
Alcuin, 91, 94
Alexander the Great, 54, 57, 68
Alfred, King, 96
Alice in Wonderland, 240
America, 179, 216, 218, 220, 235, 249
Anastatius, Emperor, 189
Anatomy of Abuses, 154
Anne of Bohemia, 113, 121
Anne of Cleves, 142
Aprons, 37, 49, 178, 197, 210
Arabia, 160
Aristotle, 54
Arkwright, Sir Richard, 217
Artemis, 52
Assur-nasir-pal, King, 37, 38
Assyria, 42
Assyrians, 35, 37, 38, 39, 59
Athens, 51, 52, 53, 54, 59
Augustine, St., 91
Autier, Leonard, 208

Babylon, 42
Babylonians, 35
Bag wigs, 193, 201, 210
Baldekyn, 106
Baldric, 114
Bands, 163, 172
Bands, standing, 166, 170
Barbette, 101
Bark cloth, 23
Bath, 197
Bavaria, 197

Bayeux Tapestry, 97
Beads, 14, 15, 31, 34, 91, 136
Beards, 32, 35, 39, 40, 62, 64, 174, 231
Beaux, 223
Beaver, 121, 174
Beefeaters, 145
Belgium, 233
Bells, 113
Belts, 28, 37, 40, 45, 46, 61, 64, 82, 92, 101, 113, 115, 129, 145, 184
Bishops, 78, 81
Black Death, 116
Black work, 157
Bloomer, Mrs. Amelia, 235, 236, 241
Bloomers, 241
Blouses, 240, 241, 243
Bluecoat boys, 145, 164
Bodices, 112, 113, 121, 139, 157, 165, 170, 171, 187, 189, 195, 198, 228
Bombast, 138, 139, 144, 165, 172, 175
Bone, 251
Bonnets, 175, 178, 220, 227, 228, 237
Books about fashion, 141
Boots, 40, 54, 58, 109, 116, 167, 218, 234, 241
Boswell, James, 212
Boudicca, 65
Bows, 169, 175, 180, 181, 195, 207
Bracco, 64, 70, 82, 89
Braid, 202, 206, 237
Breeches, 84, 88, 92, 97, 100, 101, 139, 145, 149, 169, 177, 180, 181, 201, 202, 205, 206, 210, 222, 223, 231, 240, 242, 243
Britain, 60, 62, 74, 90, 91, 93
British Museum, 93
Brittany, 167
Broad cloth, 133

INDEX

Brocade, 86, 94, 98, 215
Bronze age, 17, 25, 63
Brooches, 55, 59, 65, 70, 75, 82, 93
Brummell, George Bryan (Beau), 224
Brussels Lace, 210
Buckles, Bronze Age, 61, 62
   shoe, 187, 202
Bulla, 68
Burgundy, 129
Bustles, 194, 215, 239, 240, 241
Buttons, 113, 137, 142, 145, 148, 163,
   169, 181, 186, 187, 189, 190,
   200, 204, 206, 222, 231
Byzantine Empire, 82, 89, 176
Byzantine Emperors, 94
Byzantines, 90
Byzantium, 82, 91, 94

'Cadenette', 173
Camel's hair, 99
Camlet, 107
Canaan, 42, 43
Canes, 175, 180, 202, 223
Capes, 14, 104
Caps, 43, 61, 120, 127, 137, 140, 146,
   174, 175, 178, 199, 228, 242
Caractacus, 65
Cartwright, Dr., 217
Catacombs, 76
Catherine of Aragon, 129
Cavaliers, 176, 178
Celts, 63, 84
Cendal, 107
Ceremonial clothes, 12, 14, 71, 81, 95
Chains, gold, 145
Charlemagne, 91, 94, 95, 96
Charles I, 175, 178
   II, 179, 182, 183, 184, 186, 189
   V, 145, 147
Charms, 13, 34, 68
Chasuble, 79, 80, 85, 91, 97
Chemise, 98, 153, 187, 231
Children, clothes of, 213, 214, 215, 226,
   229, 230
China, 53, 54, 72, 83, 209, 216
Chinese, 53, 72
Chiton, Doric, 51, 52, 54, 55, 78
   Ionic, 54, 55, 70, 78
Christ, 78

Christians, 76 et seq., 91
Christ's Hospital, 145, 164
Christina, Queen of Sweden, 194
Chlamys, 56
Chopines, 162
Cinema, 249
Clavus, 69, 73, 76, 85, 86
Cleanliness, 194, 212, 224
Cloaks, 13, 63, 70, 82, 86, 88, 91, 92,
   93, 96, 97, 99, 107, 124, 131,
   144, 147, 148, 173, 189, 190,
   191, 204
Clogs, 167, 234
Clothes as decorations, 12, 13, 14
   reasons for wearing, 11-13
Cloth making, 18, 19, 20, 21, 22, 23
Cloth merchants, 117
Cloth of gold, 87, 91, 94
Clovis, 89
Coats, 41, 43, 45, 138, 182, 184, 188,
   199, 200, 202, 204, 206, 210,
   221, 223, 231, 237, 240, 246
Coats, blue, 164
Cobblers, 109, 167
Coif, 105
Collars, 31, 41, 47, 86, 103, 118, 119,
   137, 144, 145, 163, 171, 172,
   176, 177, 181, 185, 186, 187,
   204, 222, 240, 241, 246
Colobium, 76, 78
Columbus, Christopher, 147
Commodus, Emperor, 72
Commonwealth, The, 177, 178, 179
Constantine, Emperor, 78, 82
Constantinople, 82, 88, 94, 134, 176
Cope, 80, 83
Cordwainers, 108, 131
   Guild of, 108
Corsets, 139, 187, 195, 209, 213, 219,
   220, 223, 227, 239, 240, 243
Cos, 54
Costumes, tailored, 244
Cotehardie, 113
Cotte, 118, 119
Cotton, 19, 26, 27, 31, 107, 215, 216,
   217, 218, 219, 221, 233, 240,
   250, 251
Cravats, 186, 188, 203, 221, 222, 223,
   224

INDEX

Crespins, 101
Crete, 47–51, 112
Crinoline, 228, 236, 237, 238, 239, 240
Crispianus, 76, 77, 108
Crispin, 76, 77, 108
Crompton, Richard, 217
Cromwell, Oliver, 117
Cross gartering, 88, 92
Crusaders, 102, 105
Cuffs, 41, 99, 122, 124, 139, 168, 172, 176, 181, 188, 200, 202, 204, 221
Curling tongs, 96
Cuthbert, St., 91
Cycling, 241, 242, 243

Dagging, 115, 116, 124
Dalmatica, 72, 73, 74, 76, 78, 85, 86, 91, 93, 94
Damask, 106, 142
Danes, 94
Darius of Persia, 40
Deacons, 78
Demosthenes, 57
Denmark, 60, 61
Diocletian, 76
Dion Cassius, 65
Disciples, The, 78
Distaff, 19, 26
Dolls as fashion models, 195
Dorians, 51
Doublet, 129, 131, 137, 138, 139, 144, 146, 148, 150, 158, 165, 166, 167, 169
Drawers, 226
Dutch fashions, 165, 171
Dyes, 22, 31, 58, 59, 67, 152

Ebbsfleet, 91
Ecclesiastical garments, 78, 80, 91
Edward the Confessor, 97
Edward I, 110, 111
     IV, 131
     VI, 160
Egypt, 42, 43, 62, 213
Egyptians, 25–34
Elastic, 243
Eleanor, Queen, 101
Elizabeth I, 138, 154, 157, 160, 161, 163, 170, 233

Elizabeth of York, 129
Embroidery, 31, 39, 43, 53, 69, 73, 84, 85, 86, 91, 92, 111, 116, 117, 118, 127, 128, 129, 132, 137, 138, 142, 143, 144, 145, 147, 157, 167, 168, 184, 195, 206, 232
England, 91, 97, 107, 134, 140, 145, 152, 157, 160, 174, 175, 176, 177, 179, 182, 184, 186, 188, 203, 209, 210, 212, 214, 217, 220, 221, 233
English women, Dutch description of, 160
Entychianus, 76
Erasmus, 145
Ermine, 117
Ethelred II, 96
Eton suits, 243
Eugénie, Queen, 233
Euphrates, River, 42
Evelyn, John, 176, 181, 183
Eyre, Sir Simon, 127

Fabrics, woven, 23, 24, 31, 36, 43
Faience beads, 31, 62
Falling ruffs, 166, 170
Fans, 160, 175
Farthingale, 153, 157, 165, 170, 171, 172, 189, 196, 236
Feathers, 127, 129, 137, 174, 175, 225, 227
Felt, 22, 174
Fibulae, 59
Field of the Cloth of Gold, 142
Flanders, 176
Flax, 19, 20, 27, 62, 99, 156, 250
Flemish weavers, 176
Flint tools, 14, 16
Florence, 134, 176
Fontange, 193, 194, 198
Fox, George, 178
France, 63, 89, 134, 151, 155, 161, 173, 176, 179, 184, 195, 202, 204, 207, 215, 219, 220, 221, 224, 233
Franks, 88, 89
Frederick the Great, 202, 204
French Revolution, 214, 219, 226
Frieze, 133, 136
Fringes, 23, 39, 44, 45, 86, 237

INDEX

Fulling, 22, 23, 117
Fur, 87, 89, 90, 91, 103, 115, 117, 118, 122, 124, 129, 136, 137, 143, 144, 145, 172
Fustian, 107, 139, 147

Gainsborough, Thomas, 209, 215
Gaiters, 231
Games, 241, 243
Garrick, David, 209
Garters, 88, 127, 149, 151, 167
Gaul, 63, 89
Gauls, 84
Gauze, 106, 113, 220
Genoa, 134
George I, 202
    IV, 220, 224
Germany, 94, 108, 126, 142, 147, 150, 162, 172, 174, 179, 195
Gipon, 113
Girdles, 52, 55, 94, 99, 110, 113, 127, 131, 132, 134, 135
Gloves, 42, 58, 81, 94, 95, 96, 110, 163, 172, 187, 221, 224, 234, 235, 237, 247 249
Goat's hair, 91, 99
Gold, Cloth of, 87, 91, 94, 117, 142, 151, 175
Gold thread, 43, 44
Golilla, 166
Gorget, 104, 115, 116
Gowns, 107, 112, 113, 121, 132, 134, 135, 136, 137, 145, 164, 173
Great Exhibition, 235
Greece, 42, 78, 110, 212, 213, 219, 221
Greeks, 51–9, 219
Greenaway, Kate, 240
Guards, 139
Gudea, King, 36, 42
Guildhall Museum, London, 75
Gunna, 93
Gym Tunics, 243

Hairdressing, 39, 40, 49, 57, 58, 62, 63, 70, 90, 91, 96, 97, 100, 119, 120, 121, 127, 129, 159, 173, 174, 178, 193, 198, 199, 201, 207, 208, 210, 213, 214, 215, 219, 220, 222, 227, 228, 243, 248

Hairpins, 17
Hamburg, 108
Handbags, 221
Handkerchiefs, 162, 200
Hanway, Jonas, 225
Hargreaves, James, 217
Harold, King, 97
Hats, 39, 40, 49, 87, 100, 105, 115, 121, 127, 140, 147, 148, 174, 178, 180, 187, 188, 199, 202, 203, 206, 208, 210, 223, 231, 237, 242, 243, 246, 247, 248, 249
Head-dresses, 32, 39, 40, 43, 45, 46, 49, 69, 93, 121, 129, 139, 159, 160, 174, 193, 194, 198, 199, 232
Hebrews, 42, 43, 78
Heddle-rod, 22
Heels, 162, 167, 181, 211, 220
Heliogabalus, Emperor, 72
Helmets, 64, 90, 98, 105
Hemp, 99, 164
Hengist, 91
Hennin, 120, 127
Henry VI, 127, 132
    VII, 129
    VIII, 129, 137, 138, 139, 142, 145, 148
Heraldry, 105, 106
Herodotus, 32, 54
Himation, 55, 56, 57, 70, 78, 79, 83, 86
Holbein, Hans, 137, 145
Holland, 165, 167, 171
Holy Roman Empire, 94
Homer, 58, 59
Honiton, Devon, 233
Hoods, 36, 40, 98, 103, 104, 114, 115, 119, 121, 127, 133, 157, 175, 199
Hoops, 196, 213, 215, 219, 220, 236
Horn, 90, 251
Horsehair, 153
Hosa, 84, 85
Hose, 97, 101, 113, 124, 134, 135, 137, 139, 144, 146, 149, 150, 165
Houppelandes, 121, 122, 124, 128, 129
Housewives, Advice to, 164

Iceni, 65
India, 72, 215
Ionians, 51

INDEX

Iron Age, 25, 63
Isabella of France, 121
Italy, 15, 89, 134, 147, 162, 176, 194, 195, 199, 233

Jabots, 203
Jackets, 167, 180
James I, 176
    II, 186
Japanese, 72
Jerkin, 137, 148, 167, 173
Jewellery, 31, 39, 45, 46, 59, 64, 72, 82, 85, 93, 99, 117, 133, 134, 137, 142, 147, 170, 174, 175, 225, 237
    imitation, 110
John, King, 109, 111
Johnson, Dr., 209, 211, 212
Joseph, 43
Julius Caesar, 63
Jumpers, 246
Justinian, Emperor, 83

Kilt, Egypt, 28
    Scotland, 63
Kirtle, 139, 153
Knickerbockers, 242
Knitting, 160, 246
Knossos, 47

Lace, 155, 156, 166, 168, 172, 176, 179, 180, 186, 187, 189, 190, 197, 202, 209
Lacing, 99, 124, 148, 165, 171, 187, 227, 239
Lancashire, 217
Laws relating to clothes, 57, 71, 104, 110, 114, 115, 117, 126, 127, 131, 144, 148, 156, 157, 163, 179, 180, 197
Leadenhall, 127
Leather, 24, 34, 41, 49, 61, 63, 89, 90, 91, 92, 93, 95, 109, 116, 127, 163, 164, 167, 179, 218
Lee, Rev. Wm., 161, 217
Linen, 19, 26, 27, 28, 31, 55, 62, 63, 89, 91, 93, 94, 99, 101, 107, 156, 164, 173, 215, 217, 231, 233, 240, 250, 251
Liripipe, 104, 114, 115, 127

Liveries, 133, 134
Lockram, 164
London, 104, 108, 127, 135, 158, 208, 216, 218, 235
London Museum, 158
Loom, weaving, 20, 21
Lorum, 86, 94
Louis XIII, 191
    XIV, 179, 181, 182, 184, 193, 198, 207
Lovelock, 174
Ludd, Ned, 233
Luddites, 233

Macaronis, 208, 209
Marie Antoinette, Queen, 208, 212
Mary, Queen, 152, 153
Mary, Queen of Scots, 163, 174
Masks, 160, 175
Merchant Adventurers, 161
Milan, 121, 134, 176
Minos, Palace of, 47
Mittens, 187, 237
Mosaics, 74, 82, 84
Moses, 43
Motoring, 244, 249
Moustaches, 97
Muffs, 175, 187, 202, 221
Muslin, 219
Mustyrdevyllers, 135, 136
Mycenae, 47

Napoleon, Emperor, 221, 223, 224, 226
Nash, Beau, 197
National Gallery, London, 145
Neckerchief, 134
Necklaces, 14, 15, 31
Needles, prehistoric, 17, 60
Neolithic Age, 18, 25
Nero, 69
Netherlands, 147, 156, 165, 210
Nether-stocks, 149, 151
Nile valley, 42
Nollekens, Joseph, 209, 210, 211, 212
    Mrs., 210, 211
Normans, 97, 98
Norfolk jackets, 242, 243
Nylon, 250, 251

Octavius, Emperor, 69

INDEX

Old Testament, 35, 42
Ornaments, personal, 14, 15, 31
Overcoat, 144

Paenula, 70, 78, 93, 121
Paint, 14
Palestine, 42
Palla, 70, 71, 73
Pallium, 79, 80, 85, 86, 91, 94, 97
Paludamentum, 83, 84, 86, 89, 94
Paned garments, 149
Panniers, 213, 215, 219, 236
Pantalettes, 226
Pantaloons, 214, 222
Papyrus, 34
Parasols, 221, 225
Parthenon, Athens, 52
Partoffles, 162
Paston family, 132-6
Patches, 175, 190, 202
Pattens, 109, 127, 167
Patterns on fabrics, 31, 52, 53, 55, 59, 63, 74, 84
Paul, St., 78
Paul's window shoes, 116
Peasant costumes, 232
Peascod doublets, 158, 165
Pedules, 88
Penalties for wearing certain garments, 46, 131, 182
Pepys, Samuel, 183, 184, 188-91
Periwigs, 185, 187, 188, 190, 191, 192, 201, 208
Persia, 42, 53, 63, 83
Persians, 35, 40, 42, 57
Petticoat breeches, 180
Petticoats, 139, 153, 171, 173, 178, 187, 188, 189, 210, 219, 220, 227, 228, 229, 236, 240, 245
Phideas, 52
Philip II of France, 104
Phoenicians, 68
Photography, 237
Pictures, costumes in, 25, 35, 42, 74, 76
Pinafore, 240
Pins, prehistoric, 17
Pitt, William, 222
Plastics, 251
Plunderhose, 150

Pockets, 115, 175, 187, 221
Points, 137, 143
Policemen, 231
Polyvinylchloride compound (PVC), 251
Pontius Pilate, 67
Pouches, 115, 175
Powder, face, 202
Powdering, hair, 202, 208, 213, 214, 215, 222
Puritans, 177, 178
Purpoint, 131
Pytheas, 63

Quakers, 178
Queensberry, Duchess of, 197
Quizzing glasses, 224

Rank, Indications of, 12, 16, 182
Rationing, clothes, 249
Ravenna, 84
Rayon, 250
Ready-made clothes, 249
Reformation, 141
Reynolds, Sir Joshua, 209, 215
Ribbon, 134, 161, 172, 175, 179, 180, 181, 187, 203, 207, 210, 225
Richard I, 104, 111
       II, 113, 121
Riding coats, 188, 189, 204
Roman Empire, 82, 89, 94
Roman relics in London, 74
Romans, 25, 51, 63, 64, 65, 90, 93
Rome, 42, 57, 64, 65, 76, 78, 91, 94, 96, 110, 209, 212, 213
Romney, George, 215
Rosetta stone, 31
Rouge, 202
Roundheads, 178
Rousseau, Jean-Jacques, 214
Rubber, 243
Ruffles, 187, 202, 204, 209, 210, 221
Ruffs, 138, 145, 153-6, 163, 166, 170, 172, 173
Russia, 195

Sacque, 198, 210
Samite, 106
Sandals, 34, 39, 54, 61, 74, 220
Sarcinet, 106, 166

INDEX

Sashes, 167, 187

Satin, 139, 140, 172, 175, 178, 187, 206, 215, 221, 225

Saxons, 90, 91, 93, 94, 96, 97, 98, 231

Scars, 14

Segmentae, 73, 82, 84

Sewing machines, 237

Shakespeare, 175

Shaving, 32, 35

Shawl, 37, 38, 39, 44

Sheepskins, 36, 38, 39, 44

Shift, 118, 119

Shirts, 97, 135, 137, 138, 139, 142, 144, 153, 170, 180, 186, 187, 202, 204

Shirt of mail, 97

Shoemakers, 108, 127

Shoemakers' Guilds, 78

Shoes, 61, 64, 85, 88, 90, 100, 109, 116, 126, 129, 137, 139, 162, 167, 168, 178, 181, 187, 201, 211, 214, 218, 220

Shorts, 249

Shrewsbury, Duchess of, 198

Sicily, 134, 176

Silk, 53, 54, 72, 81, 83, 84, 87, 91, 93, 94, 95, 99, 100, 106, 116, 117, 132, 134, 139, 147, 149, 153, 160, 163, 167, 172, 175, 176, 178, 187, 189, 190, 206, 210, 215, 216, 221, 225, 250, 251

Silkworms, 53, 72, 83, 84, 176, 250

Silver, cloth of, 117

Silvester, Pope, 78

Skins as clothing, 13, 14, 16, 17, 18, 24, 60

Skirts, 112, 113, 171, 173, 187, 188, 198, 207, 227, 228, 229, 236, 237, 238, 240, 241, 243, 244, 245, 248

 Bronze Age, 62

 Egyptian, 30

 Sumerian, 35

Slashing, 137, 139, 144, 148, 168

Slave trade, 218

Sleeves, 40, 41, 68, 70, 73, 82, 86, 92, 94, 99, 103, 113, 121, 122, 124, 126, 137, 138, 139, 141, 144, 148, 168, 172, 180, 181, 182,

185, 188, 195, 210, 219, 221 227, 236, 241

Slippers, 135

Smocks, 93, 98, 231, 232

Soap, 194

Socca, 90, 92

Socks, 160, 168

Soldiers, Roman, 70

Sophocles, 57

Spain, 147, 151, 152, 160, 163, 165, 166, 171, 172, 179

Sparta, 51, 52

Spindle, 20, 26

Spinning, 19, 20, 26, 60, 107, 217, 232, 233

Spinning jenny, 217

 mule, 217

 wheel, 161, 217, 233

Starch, 154, 166, 228

Statues, 25, 35, 36, 47, 51, 52, 57, 58

Sterne, Lawrence, 209

Stock, 203

Stocking frame, 161

 knitting machine, 233

Stockings, 101, 113, 145, 148, 151, 160, 178, 202, 208, 210, 220, 222, 249

Stola, Roman, 70, 73

Stole, 91

Stomacher, 129, 135, 138, 157, 170, 171, 210, 250

Stone Age, Old, 15, 25

Stones, precious, 8, 86, 91, 93, 95, 109, 110, 117, 118, 128, 129, 142, 143, 157, 158, 170, 171, 175 176, 210

Straw hats, 199

Stubbs, Philip, 155

Sumerians, 35

Superstitions, 13, 110

Surcoat, 102, 115, 116, 119

Sutton Hoo treasure, 93, 94

Swiss Guard, 150

Sword belt, 167

Swords, 175, 184, 202, 210, 213, 223

Synthetic fabrics, 250

Tablion, 83, 85, 86

Tacitus, 89

Tailors, Guild of, 108

INDEX

Tanners, 109, 127
Tanning, 24, 93
Tassels, 39, 45, 87, 99
Tattooing, 14
Television, 249
Terylene, 251
Teuton tribes, 89
Theodora, Empress, 84, 85
Tierra del Fuego, 13
Tights, 219
Tigris, River, 42
Tin mining, 63
Toga, 65, 66-8, 71, 78, 86
  picta, 68, 71, 82
  praetexta, 68
Torques, 64, 91
Tortoiseshell, 251
Tower of London, 145
Trade guilds, 118, 160, 161
Trains, 99, 220, 240
Treasure from Sutton Hoo, 94
Trousers, 41, 63, 68, 82, 84, 85, 88, 89,
  90, 92, 100, 168, 169, 222, 226,
  231, 235, 236, 240, 249
Trunk hose, 139, 148, 149, 150, 152,
  165
Tudor times, 137, 146
Tunica palmata, 69, 71, 82
  talaris, 68
Tunics, 82, 84, 86, 88, 89, 90, 91, 92,
  93, 94, 96, 97, 98, 102, 107, 112,
  113, 122, 124, 231, 247
  Roman, 68, 69, 71, 72, 73
  T-shaped, 29, 30, 37, 40, 44, 51, 62,
  63, 64, 68, 72, 247
Turner, Mistress, 154
Tyre, 68
Tyrens, 47

Ulysses, 58
Umbrella, 225, 226
Under-proppers, 154
Underskirts, 139
Uniforms, 204, 205, 223, 246, 249
Upper-stock, 148
Ur, 42

Van Dyck, Anthony, 175
Veils, 93, 121, 131, 140, 159, 175, 244
Velasquez, 166
Velvet, 99, 116, 121, 129, 139, 140,
  142, 147, 172, 175, 190, 191,
  193, 209, 210, 221, 222, 237
'Venetians', 149
Venice, 134, 192, 210
Versailles, 179, 195, 196
Vest (or waistcoat), 183, 184, 185, 200
Victoria and Albert Museum, 53, 157,
  198
Victoria, Queen, 233

Waistcoat, 137, 184, 185, 186, 187, 199,
  200, 214, 215, 216, 221, 222, 231
Warmth, clothing for, 16
Warp, 20
Wars of the Roses, 124, 145
Watches, 145, 202, 206
Watteau, Antoine, 198
Weaving, 20, 21, 22, 26, 60, 107, 116,
  117, 217, 232, 233
Weft, 20
Wesley, John, 209
West, Benjamin, 212
Westminster Abbey, 113
Whorl, spindle, 20
Wife, instructions to, 118, 119
Wigs, 32, 160, 181, 185, 187, 188, 190,
  191, 192, 193, 201, 202, 215
William the Conqueror, 97
Wimple, 101, 115, 119, 120
Wool, 19, 26, 27, 31, 35, 42, 51, 55, 61,
  62, 63, 73, 89, 90, 91, 99, 107,
  117, 160, 218, 219, 240, 250, 251
Wool merchants, 107, 116

Xenophon, 42

Yeomen of the Guard, 145, 172

Zeus, 57